THE JOYVILLE SWEAT SOX

LINDA FAUSNET

Published by Wannabe Pride 2015

Editing by Katreina Knights

Cover Design by Chuck DeKett

FIRST EDITION.

Library of Congress Control Number: 2015939700

❀ Created with Vellum

For Noah Fausnet.
You'll always be my favorite baseball player.

1

It's against the law to get mad in Joyville.

Can you believe that? Of all the stupid, idiotic, ridiculous— No. I gotta stop. That's how I got into all this trouble in the first place. I stuffed a piece of gum in my mouth because chewing gum helps me keep calm. Sometimes.

The judge grinned at me. Judge Terrance Mann, or "The Judge Mann" as he's known in Joyville, hates me. He lowered his head and peered at me over his glasses. He was a really big dude. You didn't realize how huge he was until he stood up from behind the bench. He had dark skin and dark eyes and tried to look scary, but I wasn't afraid of him. Okay, I might have been a little afraid of what he was going to say. He loved his precious little Joyville, and he thought my bad attitude messed up his perfect little town. Hey, I love the town, grew up here, and couldn't imagine living anywhere else. I'm just not the type that can be all happy-smiley-goody-goody all the time. So sue me. Well, the judge wasn't suing me. He had something much, much worse in mind.

"Konstance MacDonald," The Judge Mann said in his annoying, loud, judgy voice. "You have broken the No Anger Law for the third and final time."

Ah, yes. His beloved No Anger Law. It might as well be called Konnie's Law, because The Judge Mann created it because of me. He fancied himself this big, important guy, and he expected everybody to treat him like he was the king of the universe or something. I guess he was pretty big and important because he was the judge for all the towns in the county, and he made all the laws. Anyway, I'm not the calmest person on the planet, and I guess he caught me on a bad day. He was lecturing me on my bad attitude, and I might have told him to get out of my way. I also might have mentioned the fact that he looked like a girl in his judge robes. He told me I made the whole town of Joyville look bad when I got angry, and I told him there was no law against getting mad.

Yeah.

There was now.

Pop! I snapped my gum so loudly that it echoed throughout the whole courtroom. The Judge Mann's lip twitched, which meant I was making him mad. Good. I loved trying to make him break his own No Anger Law. I flipped my shoulder-length blonde hair back and out of my face. I hated wearing my hair down, but I figured I had to look halfway decent in court. I couldn't wait to pull my hair back into a ponytail the way I normally wore it.

"You've been a problem in this town for twenty-one years now, little missy," he said.

Pop!

"Twenty-one and a half, Judge," I told him. Actually, that wasn't even true. I mean, yeah, I'm twenty-one years old, but I wasn't always a problem. I used to be a pretty nice kid for a while. Then some bad stuff happened when I was sixteen, and I guess that's when I got a little mean.

"You've been more than a little mean, lately," The Judge Mann said, as if he were reading my mind. "You've always had an awful temper problem, but this was really the last straw."

Pop!

"Aw, come on. It wasn't that bad."

"A screaming argument with the ice cream man? You shouted at him that the ice cream was too cold." He leaned on his arm and peered down at me over his glasses again.

I shrugged. "It was. Sensitive teeth," I said, then tapped my front teeth with my finger. The Judge Mann squinted at me as if he were trying to vaporize me with a laser beam from his eyes.

"You then proceeded to smash your ice cream cone onto the top of his head, telling him, quote, 'If you think it's so warm, why don't you wear it as a hat?'" He narrowed his eyes even further. It almost looked like he was asleep.

I grinned as giggles rippled throughout the courtroom. The Judge Mann's eyes flew open wide as he silenced everyone with a look. An angry look. Which is against the Joyville law. Must be nice to be the judge.

"This latest outburst, sadly, leaves me no choice but to sentence you to five years in jail."

Sadly. Puh-leeeze. He didn't look sad. I sighed heavily, but I knew it was coming. That was the law. If you lost your temper three times in less than a year, then you went to jail.

"Wait!" someone shouted as he burst through the door. We all turned around to see that it was Gabe Steinbrenner, the wealthiest and most powerful man in the town of Joyville. I wondered what he wanted. Much as I'd have liked to believe he was here to rescue me from prison, I knew he was way too selfish for that. He only cared about himself and his precious reputation. Gabe was an old guy. In his fifties, at least. He loved to wear fancy stuff like expensive suits, gold watches, and even rings. He also expected to be treated like the king of the universe, just like The Judge Mann.

Gabe went running up to the judge and started whispering in his ear. Everybody else in the courtroom started whispering to each other about his whispering. I looked around, kinda wishing I had somebody to whisper to.

The Judge Mann didn't look happy about whatever Gabe Steinbrenner was telling him. I hoped maybe I would finally get to see him lose his temper in front of all these people. "A-HA!" I would shout. "You broke the law! Off to prison with *you*!"

The Judge Mann sighed heavily, and then nodded. He might not like whatever Mr. Steinbrenner told him, but he clearly wasn't going to argue with him about it. Darn.

"Instead of going to jail," the judge said, "I have another choice for you."

"Really?" I asked him. No way! I thought I was gonna be a jailbird for sure.

"Really, Miss MacDonald," he said, speaking through clenched teeth. "Mr. Steinbrenner has offered you another option instead of going to jail."

Mr. Steinbrenner held up two thumbs like a giant dork. Oh, man. I already knew exactly what this "other option" was going to be. He'd been trying to get me to agree to coach his new baseball team all year. The guy had never had any interest in baseball, and he probably still didn't. He just couldn't stand Bobby Hearsay, the most powerful man in the nearby town of Cranksville. Bobby bragged and bragged about how perfect and wonderful and awesome his baseball team was, and it made Gabe Steinbrenner nuts. Gabe and Bobby used to be best buddies back in college. That is, until Bobby stole Gabe's girlfriend. Bobby told the girl Gabe had an evil twin named Kabe, and that the two were always switching and she would never know which one she was going out with. It was totally not true, but the girl was about as bright as a candle in a windstorm, so she believed it.

Since his enemy, Bobby, had a super-wonderful baseball team, now Gabe had to have an even better one. It made me really mad (but then, what doesn't?) that Mr. Steinbrenner suddenly developed an interest in baseball just because Bobby was all into it. Gabe had always been way into football. He had never cared about baseball. He had no respect for the game, which was why I had no respect for him. And now he had to have his own baseball team of a bunch of eleven-and twelve-year-olds, and he wanted me, Konnie Mack, to coach them.

Well, of course he wanted me to coach the team. I'm the best baseball player this town has ever seen, and he knew it. Everyone knew it. But I don't play anymore. Not since Bobby Hearsay left Joyville. I'll never forgive him for what he did for as long as I live. Bobby took all Joyville's baseball teams with him when he left for Cranksville. Snuck them out in the middle of the night.

It was awful. My dad and I were completely devastated. My dad taught me to love the game of baseball. And I do love it. With all my heart. I also love my dad with all my heart. He died the same year Bobby Hearsay stole baseball from Joyville when I was only sixteen. My poor dad spent the last summer of his life in and out of the Joyville hospital. His favorite thing to do in the whole world was to go to baseball games, and in his last summer alive there was no baseball in Joyville. Nothing would have made him happier than to go see some baseball games with me on steamy summer afternoons or balmy summer nights. Instead, he was really sad that baseball was gone. Then he died.

And that's when I got mad.

Neither Gabe nor The Judge Mann did anything to stop Bobby Hearsay from stealing the team, and I guess I never really forgave either one of them. But now, after all this time, baseball was coming back to Joyville.

So my choice came down to this: go to jail for five years or spend one summer coaching the game of baseball; the game I love more than anything else in the world. It would mean coaching a bunch of bratty kids; kids who knew absolutely zero about baseball because they'd never even seen a game played in their town. I pictured myself on the field, trying to teach a bunch of clueless, loudmouthed preteens who wouldn't know a baseball if it hit them in the head. Which it probably would. Repeatedly. And I might be the one throwing it.

"So which is it going to be, Miss MacDonald? Five years in the Joyville prison or coach Mr. Steinbrenner's new baseball team for a few months?"

Pop!

"Jail," I said.

2

Fine, fine. Of course, I chose coaching the kids instead of going to jail. I just had to think about it, that's all. Sure, dealing with those kids would be far, far worse than any jail term could ever be, but it came down to simple math. A few months in the summer was a lot shorter than five years in the slammer.

Plus, being able to weasel out of my jail sentence totally annoyed The Judge Mann, which was an added bonus. Boy, was he mad. He was positively giddy when I'd lost my temper for the third time and he thought he could finally toss me in a cell. Not today, pal.

"Konstance MacDonald, you are hereby sentenced to community service. You must coach the Joyville Sweat Sox for the summer," The Judge Mann said.

That was cool, I guess. It was only one summer. Plus, all he said was I had to coach the little buggers. He didn't say they actually had to *win* anything.

"However," he continued, looking down at me all judgmental-like, "If you get angry even *once*, you will go to jail and serve out your full five years. Do you understand?"

Pop! went my gum. Five years in jail was beyond ridiculous. It was probably the harshest punishment you could get for anything in Joyville, and he did it just to spite me. The punishment for stealing a car was cleaning the judge's house, for the love of Pete Rose! The Judge Mann made all sorts of nutso laws, like making his own birthday a town holiday. Well, that one wasn't so bad. We all liked having the day off.

"Oh, yeah. Sure thing. Whatever," I told him.

"That means no yelling, no screaming, no raising your voice—"

"Isn't that all kinda the same thing? Yelling and screaming and raising your voice?"

The Judge Mann blinked at me. He was probably trying really hard not to yell or scream or raise his voice.

"I suppose. Still, it means no hollering, no fighting, no launching frozen desserts at people's heads…"

I thought about asking him, "*What about warm desserts, like hot apple pie or freshly baked gingerbread*?" I decided not to push my luck.

"Yes, Judge. I understand. Coach the kids. No getting mad. Got it."

Pop! went my gum.

Bam! Went The Judge Mann's gavel, making my punishment official.

Thunk! I set down my heavy bag of baseball equipment on the Johnny Bench. I took a deep breath as I looked out over the baseball field. The air smelled so good, so fresh. That scent of dirt and grass and summer sunshine. Well, okay, you can't *smell* sunshine, but you know what I mean. That special smell of summer that makes you feel like anything is possible.

I stood at home plate and looked across the diamond. The warm, gentle wind blew through my hair. I closed my eyes, remembering all the times I had played the game. Sliding into second base, grinding the dirt into my nice, white pants. The firm feel of home plate under my feet as I crossed over it to score a run. The satisfying *Thwack*! of connecting with the baseball, launching it all the way to center field.

I hadn't been on a baseball field since I was sixteen years old. I felt a dull ache in my chest, like I could feel an empty spot in my heart. A spot that was once filled with baseball dreams and maybe could be filled again. I also felt that empty hole in my heart from my dad that couldn't ever be filled. I missed him so much.

Remembering my passion for baseball, I was excited about this coaching thing for a second. Just for a second, but then I came to my senses. Yeah, I might get to play baseball again, but this time it would be with a bunch of kids who didn't know a thing about the game. After all, they grew up in a town that hadn't had a baseball team in their lifetime. Mr. Steinbrenner didn't care about the game. He just wanted to beat old Bobby Hearsay's team. Still, he had done a nice job getting the field ready after all these years.

There was no mud in Joyville. He had to send Mighty Casey, the maintenance guy, over to Cranksville to truck in the dirt for the field. Mighty Casey was kind of an odd dude. He was really nice, though. Always had a smile and wave. He was skinny and about as tall as a redwood tree, so most people just called him The Giant.

The field looked amazing, but I sure wished it had a better name. Our home field was named after the company that paid for it: the Law Offices of Sorkin, Effrey, and Roberts. It's not a good sign that those initials spell out L.O.S.E.R. That's right, folks. The Joyville Sweat Sox played at L.O.S.E.R. field.

The first loser—I mean player—showed up ten minutes early. His mom dropped him off and didn't even come over to say hello. She just kinda shot me a suspicious look before she drove off. I guess some parents weren't too crazy about the idea of a convicted criminal coaching their kids. Whatever.

"Hi," the little dude said to me. "I'm Clueless Joe Jackson."

"Are you serious?" I asked him. What the heck kind of name was Clueless? I guess a kid with that name would fit right in here at L.O.S.E.R. Field.

He nodded and said, "Nice to meetcha." He had light brown hair, brown eyes, and freckles all over his face. He had a friendly smile. He was a cute little fella, I guess.

"Why on earth do people call you Clueless Joe?"

"Well," Clueless said, as he leaned down and pulled up the black knee-high socks that had fallen down around his ankles. "One time I was playin' outside with my friends and my shoes were new and too tight and stuff, so I took 'em off and just ran around in my socks." He glanced down at his black socks. "These used to be white...so, anyway, people just started calling me Clueless Joe since I didn't wear shoes."

"Oh, I see," I said. "No, I don't. Wait a minute. What? Why do people call you Clueless Joe instead of—"

"The name Shoeless Joe was already taken by some other old guy a long time ago," he explained.

"That makes sense," I said, even though it made no sense whatsoever.

"Hi," came a voice from right behind me.

"Bah!" I yelped. "You scared the heck outta me."

"Sorry," the kid said, shrugging. "I'm Catfish. Catfish Punter." He extended his hand like a grown-up would, and I shook it firmly. He had blond hair and was tall and pretty muscular for a kid. He might actually be a decent ballplayer. A power hitter or maybe a pitcher.

"Nice to meet you, Catfish," I told him. It took every ounce of self-control I had not to make fun of his name. It was almost painful for me not to ask, *Where are your whiskers, Catfish? Were your parents on a fishing trip when they came up with that? You're lucky your name isn't Tackle Box or Fishing Hook.* Nope. I behaved and didn't say a single word. But man, it wasn't easy.

A grouchy-looking girl showed up next. Her equally grouchy-looking father brought her.

"So you're Konstance MacDonald," Mr. Grouchy Dad said.

"You can call me Konnie Mack," I told him. I already didn't like the guy. He was definitely the sporty type, as he wore a Joyville football jersey and looked like he lifted weights. He was bald on top and had a moustache and a beard. He was a tough-looking guy. I wondered how many times he'd lost his temper lately, and if he'd ever been caught by The Judge Mann.

Grouchy Dad waggled a finger in my face. "You better be niiiiice. Wouldn't want you to get mad or anything!" He winked at me, and I wanted to punch him. So, I guess the parents were fully aware of how I ended up with this coaching gig. I shouldn't be surprised. My arrest and sentencing were in all the local newspapers.

"Well, I gotta go," Grouchy Dad said. *Good. I won't miss you.*

"Why are you leaving?" his daughter asked, looking disappointed. She had brown eyes, short, sassy brown hair, and wore jeans and a ripped sweatshirt. I got the feeling she was going for the tough-guy look just like her father. It's hard to look tough when you're sad, though.

"Ty," he said, grinning. "I gotta go see your brother at football practice. You understand. I mean, this is just baseball," he said, dismissing the field with his hand.

Just baseball? Lucky for him, I wasn't allowed to get mad. Cause if I had been, he'd have been flat on his back with my knuckleprint stamped on his cheek.

"Yeah, okay," the girl said quietly. She didn't look like it was okay. I could see her fighting to hold back tears.

"Oh, she's Tyler Corncobb, by the way," her dad said with the same dismissive wave as he had with the baseball field. Like he was saying *this is just my daughter.* He winked at her. "Don't come home a failure!" He jumped in his car and sped off.

Ty was back to scowling. She stared at me so I stared right back at her. We stared at each other for what felt like ten minutes. It was weird. But neither one of us wanted to be the first to look away.

Suddenly, what looked like a blur of arms and flying hair came whooshing right between us. Ty and I stared in astonishment as the latest teammate to arrive did four cartwheels in a row before finally stopping and running back up to us.

"Hi!" she shouted perkily into my face. "I'm Joanna. Joanna Demargio. People call me Joltin' Joanna!"

"I can't imagine why." I said. The girl acted like someone had zapped her with a bolt of electricity. She shifted her feet back and forth, back and forth. I was getting motion sickness just watching her. Joanna had her long, dark brown hair tied back with a blue ribbon that kept swaying with her constant movement. "Nice to meet you," I lied. Jeez, what a nut.

Two more girls arrived on the scene. The first girl looked more like a cheerleader than a ballplayer. She had perfectly painted pink nails and bright blond hair. She wore rings, necklaces, bracelets, and earrings—basically, she'd hung something from every part of her body that she possibly could.

"I'm Brooke," she said daintily. "Brooke Robinson." Then she curtsied. She actually *curtsied.* Yikes.

The other girl didn't look a whole lot more promising. She was a pretty girl with brown skin and friendly brown eyes, but she wore pigtails. Pigtails are great. Pigtails are cute. If you're in kindergarten. Or, you know, if you're a pig.

"Hi! I'm Christy Mathews," she said. I nodded at her, grateful that she didn't curtsey or bow. I had to stifle the urge to yank on one of those pigtails.

I looked up to see another dad approaching. Great. I wasn't so thrilled with the last player's dad, and I wasn't looking forward to meeting another one. It was weird, though. This dad didn't seem to have a kid with him. As he got closer, I realized why.

He *was* the kid. And he was taller than me.

He couldn't have been older than twelve, or he wouldn't have been allowed on the team, but holy home runs, he looked like he was at least sixteen. I wondered if he needed to shave yet. He had brown hair, blue eyes, and a friendly smile.

"Hi! My name's Carl Repkin, Jr. and I haven't changed my underwear in 2,130 days," he informed me.

I just blinked at him. *What?*

"Figured I went this far, I might as well go for the record."

"I, um. I'm not sure what to do with that information. Um...thanks?" I said uncertainly.

"Sure thing!" he said, grinning at me. His size was somewhat intimidating, but he did have a friendly face. I hoped his size and Catfish's toughness would somehow counteract Brooke's and Christy's girlishness and make our team look at least halfway competitive. Hey, I got nothing against girls. I am one, as I recall. But you gotta be tough if you're gonna play sports. I didn't need Brooke throwing a hissy fit if she broke a nail, or Christy getting all bent out of shape if her pigtails got crooked while she chased a line drive.

"Oooh, I almost forgot. I baked brownies!" Carl said with enthusiasm as he used his giant hands to pull a glass pan of brownies from his bag.

"Thanks!" came a muffled voice. His voice was muffled because he somehow already had a mouthful of Carl's brownies. "Hi," the kid said, his mouth still full. "I'm George. George Ruthenbabe."

Wow. This kid seemed to have appeared out of nowhere. He had light brown skin and was, shall we say, pleasingly plump. He seemed to have a built-in radar where snacks were involved. One mention of brownies, and he seemed to have emerged from the mist in the outfield.

"Nice to meet you," I said, lying again. This kid was not going to be lightning-quick on the basepaths. "Ooookay. Who are we missing here? So far, we've got Catfish Punter, Clueless Joe Jackson, Ty Corncobb, Joltin' Joanna Demargio, Brooke Robinson, Carl Repkin, Jr., Christy Mathews, George Ruthenbabe...we're missing one. Yoyo? Yoyo Beara?"

"I'm here," whispered a cute little Asian kid. Apparently, he'd been hiding behind George Ruthenbabe. Hiding behind George was like hiding behind a brick building. "I've been talking to you for five minutes," he said, still whispering.

"Nice to..." I started to whisper, but then realized I was on a baseball field, not in a library. I spoke louder, probably louder than necessary. "Nice to meet you. Yoyo, is it? Why do they call you Yoyo?"

"Probably as in Yo! Yo! Speak up, man!" Catfish said, making the other kids laugh. Yoyo just shrugged but didn't look particularly upset.

"Okay, let's get started here," I said, looking over my ragtag group.

Pop! Went my gum.

This was going to be a really long season.

I don't know. Maybe it wouldn't be as bad as it looked.

"So!" said Joltin' Joanna brightly. "Where's all the rackets?"

Nope. It won't be as bad as I thought. It was gonna be much, much worse.

"Rackets?" I asked.

"You know," Joanna said, swatting an imaginary racket in the air. Then she did three cartwheels.

I took a deep breath and spoke calmly. "There are no rackets in baseball. We use bats, dear. Baseball bats. Rackets are for tennis."

"Oh, right," said Carl, startling me with that deep, tough voice of his. I still couldn't believe the kid was only twelve. "That's tennis. This is baseball. The one with the hoops." With that, he swished an imaginary basketball in the air.

"Um, no. No, actually, that's basketball," I said. Carl should know. He was tall enough to play for the New York Knicks.

"Right, right," George Ruthenbabe chimed in, his mouth

still full of brownies. "But where's the goal net doohickey thingamabob?"

I rubbed my temples, feeling a severe headache coming on. "No, no, sweetie," I said through clenched teeth. "That's hockey."

"Yeah, that's hockey. No net, no pucks," said little Clueless. "This is the one with the little ball, like this big." He made a circle with his hand that was about the size of a baseball. Relief flooded through me. *Finally.* "You know, it's the hard, rubbery ball that you catch in the little stick with the net thingy on the end."

I sighed deeply. I took in several breaths to keep from completely flipping out. "No, no. That's lacrosse."

"I'll help you go get the clubs," Christy said, twirling her pigtails as she headed toward the dugout.

"Golf," I said simply, resisting the urge to have a full-out temper tantrum right there on the field. I was about to lose it, but I knew I couldn't. I wasn't allowed to.

"You've all got it all wrong," said Brooke, examining her painted fingernails. "All we need is a football."

"No!" I said sharply. "Football is for football! That's why it's called a football! Are you kidding me with this?"

The kids just stared at me. Oops. I was pretty sure none of them was aware of my legal problems, but they still might run home and tattle that I had gotten angry at practice. I needed to chill out.

"That is, you know, " I said in a sickeningly sweet voice, "A football is called a football because that's the name of the sport, ya know?" Ty arched an eyebrow and looked at me warily. I didn't think she was buying my sweet and innocent act. "This game is called *baseball* so we use a *baseball* to play it." Holy home runs, I could not believe I actually had to explain that to them.

"Yeah," whispered Yoyo. "That's what I've been trying to say. We need a baseball, a bat, and a glove."

I looked at Yoyo. Jeez, he was like Einstein compared to these other kids. But it wouldn't matter that the kid was a genius if you couldn't hear a single word he was saying!

"Um, yes. Yes, exactly! Feel free to, you know..." I stopped myself before I said, *Feel free to speak like a real person and not like Casper the Friendly Ghost.* "You know, speak up so everybody can hear you!" I managed a smile.

Yoyo shrugged and whispered, "Okay."

Yikes. I give up.

Joltin' Joanna started doing cartwheels in the infield. Brooke and Christy were chatting and comparing makeup notes. Carl started discussing his brownie recipe with George while Catfish argued with Yoyo about his whispering. I realized I had to get some control here.

"Okay!" I said loudly. "I think we better get started with some ground rules." I headed toward the dugout, then realized no one was following me. "Come with me, team. Please." Sheesh. I realized I was gonna have to spell out every single thing I wanted them to do. *Don't forget to breathe, now.*

I took them into the little locker room inside the dugout. I had put pieces of masking tape with their names written on them on their lockers. I was almost afraid I was going to have to show each one of them to their lockers, but they seemed to be able to read. Thank goodness. They even sat on the bench and faced me without being asked, so that was something, I guess.

I picked up a black dry-erase marker and wrote in big letters on the whiteboard: CODE OF CONDUCT!!! The kids were back to chattering, but I silenced them by clearing my throat loudly.

"Code of Conduct Rule #1." I began writing as I spoke. "No One Talks When the Coach is Talking." I turned around to look at the kids. They were silent. "Good job." They all grinned at me, pleased with themselves. They were kinda sweet, I guess.

"Rule #2. You Will Always be in the Appropriate Uniform for Games and Practices." I underlined the word "appropriate" three times. I turned back to face them. "That means baseball jersey, pants, cleats, and cap." I thought for a minute, realizing I might need to be even more specific. "That means no hockey masks, no tennis shorts, no football helmets. Okay?"

"Hey, coach?" A little voice said. I felt like groaning, but I didn't. I wanted to get through this as quickly and painlessly as possible. I turned back around, my marker still poised in my hand ready to write the next rule. It was little Clueless Joe, sitting there with his hand politely in the air. My anger softened a bit. I couldn't help it. He was a cute little guy.

"Yes?"

"Um, we don't have uniforms yet." He looked a little worried. "At least I don't."

I smiled at him, feeling my anger disappear completely, replaced with an unfamiliar but warm feeling in my stomach. You couldn't be mad at this kid. You just couldn't. He was adorable. "No, hon. You're right," I said softly. "We didn't get the uniforms in yet, but hopefully by the next practice. The Joyville Sweat Sox are sponsored by Dizzy Dean's Paint Supply, and they should be sending us uniforms soon." I winked at him and he smiled, looking relieved. "And speaking of uniforms..." I turned again to write on the board. "Rule #3. Everyone Will Take Turns Doing the Team's Laundry. When you see a red tag in your locker, that means it's your turn to do the laundry."

"Um, coach?" Carl Repkin, Jr. said. "About my underwear..."

"What? Oh, right. That weird—ah, I mean, right. That, you know, amazing streak you have going with not changing your underwear. Yeah, that's great. You don't have to wash your underwear," I said, trying not to wince. Yuck-o. *Whatever.*

"Rule #4," I continued. "You Will Pay Attention and Learn the Rules of the Game." I felt like groaning just thinking about how much work it was going to be to teach them to play baseball. They might as well all be nicknamed "Clueless" from what I'd witnessed so far. They didn't seem to know the first thing about the sport. "Rule #5. You Will Always Do Your Best and Try Your Hardest."

I looked over my list and sighed. My list looked kinda, well, a little mean, I guess. So I added "Rule #6. Always Be a Team Player." I added that one because it sounded like something a coach was supposed to say. I saved the most important rule for last. I turned around to face them. I wanted them to hear the final rule before I wrote it down. I wanted them to know how serious I was. I wanted them to see it in my eyes.

"Rule #7," I said firmly, trying to make eye contact with each one of them. "You will respect the game of baseball." Nine pairs of eyes stared at me solemnly. They all nodded. I turned to write the rule on the board. I wrote in all capital letters.

YOU WILL RESPECT THE GAME OF BASEBALL.

I put the marker down. It was time to get to work.

3

I took the kids onto the field. I was tired just thinking about the uphill battle ahead of me. Baseball's a great game, but there are a lot of rules and it was a little harder to learn than, say, basketball. I mean, swish. Put large ball into basket and we're good to go. There was a lot more to baseball. I figured I'd better start with something simple.

"Okay, let's get our gloves on and we'll start by tossing the ball around a bit." The kids grabbed their gloves and most of them put them on their right hands. Hmmm. Either I had an unusually large number of left-handed kids on my team, or they were putting the gloves on wrong.

"Okay, everybody. Let's make sure we're putting the gloves on the right—I mean *correct*—hands. If you're right-handed, then the glove goes on your left hand."

"Well, that's a dumb rule. It makes no sense," Catfish said gruffly.

"It does too make sense," I said. "You want to catch the ball in your glove, but you want to throw with your dominant hand. If you do everything else, like write or turn a doorknob or pick your nose with your right hand, then that's the hand you want to throw with."

"Heh heh," Catfish chuckled. "That's funny. Turn a doorknob..."

I just rolled my eyes. I picked up my own glove and slid it on my left hand. I caught a whiff of the leather smell. I was seized by the memory of how I used to feel playing this game. How I loved the smell of leather. The feel of the ball in my glove. It was so good to be back on a baseball field. It had been far too long.

"Okay, let's get started. Somebody toss the ball."

"Cool!" Christy said enthusiastically. Then she gently, slowly, rolled the ball over to Brooke. Yikes. I grabbed some chewing gum.

Pop! Ahh. That's better.

"This isn't bowling, Christy. We don't roll the ball. Toss it. Like this." I tossed the ball over to her, and she dropped to the ground like she was avoiding a nuclear missile strike. She'd never make it out on the field if she hit the deck every time a ball came near her. Better stick her in the outfield. "Um, I think you'd make a great right fielder." Christy nodded happily.

"Oooh!" Joltin' Joanna shouted. "I wanna play side field!"

I sighed wearily. "There is no such thing as 'side field,' dear. It's right field, left field, or center field." No way. That girl had way too much energy to be wasted in the outfield. Besides, if you gave her that much room out there, she'd just turn cartwheels the whole darn game. "I think you'd be great at second base." The girl was fast, and a lot of balls would get hit to second base. She nodded happily and dashed off to the outfield.

"Joanna! Second base. Second. One, two..." I said, pointing at second base. She saluted and did cartwheels in the general direction of second base. She got there. Eventually.

"I wanna be quarterback!" Catfish shouted.

"I call goalie!" Carl yelled.

I felt like lying down on the field and taking a nap. I did not have the mental energy to even begin to explain about baseball positions.

"Put me in, coach!" Brooke said brightly. "I'm ready today. To play!"

"Okay, okay. Calm down, everybody. Everyone will get a position. Let me just, you know, watch you for a bit so I can figure out what you're good at and we'll go from there." *I'll figure out what you stink at and how to minimize the damage. That's how I'll choose positions.* "Let's just practice a little here."

I picked up a baseball and tossed it up and down a couple of times, catching it in my glove.

"Wow," Christy said.

Wow was right. These kids were easily impressed.

"Okay, now I'm gonna toss it over to some of you. Just do the best you can to catch it in your glove. Ready?" They all nodded eagerly. I had to admit I liked seeing their enthusiasm. They might not know squat, but they seemed to want to learn. I tossed the ball casually over to Yoyo.

He caught it neatly in his glove.

I about fell over in shock.

"Wow. Nice job, Yoyo!"

"If you throw it...I will catch it," he whispered.

"Okay, you can be the catcher," I told him. He nodded. He might have said something, but who could tell with that guy? "All right. I'm gonna throw to somebody else." The kids all looked at me, nodding.

I tossed the ball over in Catfish's direction. His right hand shot up and he nabbed the ball out of the air.

"Ow!" he shouted. "That hurts!"

I winced. "With your *glove,* Catfish. Use the glove. That's what it's for. Barehanding the ball hurts. That's why you've got this gigantic glove on your other hand!" He looked at me all wide-eyed and innocent. I felt bad for yelling. He could have hurt himself. "I mean, that's good! That's good you showed us what not to do. Catching the ball with your bare hand hurts, so now we know, right? Lesson learned!"

Catfish grinned broadly, which actually made me feel pretty good. I realized the more these kids laughed and smiled, the less stressed out I was. I didn't mean to yell at them. It was just a habit of mine. A bad habit. These kids were sweet and they didn't deserve to be yelled at. They weren't the ones who took baseball away from me and my dad. They were the ones who were bringing it back.

"Okay, let's try again with somebody else." I looked over in Brooke's direction. She was looking at her nails, as usual. Well, I had to give everyone a turn so I might as well get it over with. In my irritation with her super-girly, non-athletic attitude, I threw the ball a lot harder than I meant to. She gasped and dashed for it and made a spectacular grab, with her glove and everything.

I just stared at her, my mouth open. Holy home runs, that was amazing!

"Brooke, that was outstanding!"

Brooke shrugged shyly. I decided to try again, to see if it was just a lucky catch. Without warning, I fired the ball again. She barely blinked as she caught it effortlessly.

Wow. *Cool.*

"Brooke, I think you would make a great third baseman. I mean lady. Third baselady. Girl. Whatever," I said. She smiled and nodded. And headed toward second base. “Third,” I reminded her gently. “Third base.”

I looked over at George. I really, really didn’t want to know how many brownies he’d eaten so far today. I was pretty sure he’d be slow as a ballplayer due to his, umm, somewhat generous size. It was probably best to stick him in center field where he could just stand still and catch balls without running too much. Then again, I’d thought Brooke was gonna be a total powder puff but it turned out she was kinda awesome at fielding.

“Head’s up!” I said as I tossed the ball over to George. He licked chocolate off his fingers as he watched the ball sail over his head. It landed in the grass. He wandered lazily over to pick it up. “Center field,” I said wearily.

Clueless Joe wandered over to left field. “I think I’ll just stand over here,” he said.

“Umm, okay,” I said. That was easy. “You’re left fielder. All right, Ty, Catfish, and Carl. I wanna see what kinda arms you got.” All three of them held up their arms for me to see. I found myself laughing instead of getting mad for once. “No, I mean, your throwing arms. Follow me.”

I walked over to the back of the dugout wall.

“Now, just throw the ball like this,” I said, as I pitched the ball as hard as I could at the wooden dugout wall. It made a satisfying *Thwap*! noise. Man, that felt good. I had missed throwing the ball around.

“Cool! Lemme try!” Carl said. I tossed the ball over to him. It hit him in the chest. “Ow!” I held up my glove, reminding him of what to do. “Oh, yeah. Right.”

He cocked back his arm and pitched the ball. It didn’t come close to reaching the dugout.

“Good try, good try!” I said as I picked up the ball. I was

impressed with my ability to lie politely without rolling my eyes at him.

"My turn," Ty said in a tough voice. She actually came over and snatched the ball out of my hand. I didn't know whether to be angry or impressed. It was kinda cool having a tough guy on the team, even if she happened to be a girl. She cocked back her arm and pitched the ball. It didn't make it to the wall, but it was really close. Not a bad throw at all, really, especially for a first try. She gritted her teeth, looking very upset with herself. "Darnit!"

"Hey, that wasn't bad," I said. Wow. I think I actually meant it that time.

Ty turned toward me, fire in her eyes. "Yes, it was. It was awful."

"Well, then try it again," I told her, retrieving the ball and tossing it to her. She caught it easily. "Nice catch," I said. She rolled her eyes at me. My temper started to flare. There was room for one angry female on this team, and I wasn't about to give up my spot. It wasn't fair. Kids couldn't be thrown in jail for getting mad like the adults could. I scowled right back at her. She cocked back her arm and fired the ball again. This time it did hit the wall. Barely. It made a weak *tap* sound when it hit.

"Hey, that was pretty good," Carl told her. Ty glanced over at him. She didn't smile, but she didn't glare at him or roll her eyes.

"I don't wanna be a pitcher anyway," Ty said. She glared fiercely at me. "First base. I wanna play first base. My dad said that's the hardest position, so that's what I want to play."

She had such a look of determination in her eyes that I figured she might actually be good at it. Besides, I was kind of afraid to tell her no.

"Fine. You're first base. All right, Catfish. Your turn." Catfish was a big dude, so I was curious to see how strong his arm was. Then again, Carl was as big as my Uncle Harold and he stunk at pitching. Carl, I mean. Not Uncle Harold.

Catfish cocked back his arm. I held my breath, hoping for a miracle. The ball rocketed forward from his arm like it had been shot out of a cannon. No doubt about it. Catfish had a really powerful throwing arm! But his aim was a little off. He missed the wall. *He missed the wall.* He threw the ball halfway to center field, which was totally awesome, but he couldn't hit the wall! That's like bouncing a rubber ball and missing the floor. How had he even managed it? He was standing right in front of it!

I just stared at him, not sure whether to be impressed or to laugh. He stared back at me with an equally questioning expression.

"Okay. Let's try that again. Little help?" I said, motioning toward the kids standing on the field. They just looked at each other, having no idea what I wanted. "The ball. Throw the ball back to me."

They all snapped to attention and ran to fetch the ball. Then they slammed into each other, their bodies bouncing back like they were made of springs. They collapsed on the field, giggling.

"Hey!" I said sharply. "You're not respecting the game. Rule #7. You will respect the game of baseball."

They slowly got up, nodding somberly. Brooke threw the ball back to me. I threw it to Catfish, who actually caught it. He pitched the ball toward the dugout. It went completely over the wall and back into center field.

I stood there staring at him. I wondered if it was too late to choose jail.

4

Wearily, I drove back to my apartment, which was nestled snugly between Mr. 3000's car dealership and Tinker's to Ever's to Chance to Dream Mattress Outlet. Not exactly a quiet space, but it was all mine. I loved being able to drive past my old school and the old ball fields where I used to play. So many memories of my dad here in Joyville. Happy memories.

The only bad thing was the number of stupid shopping malls that kept cropping up all over the place, crowding out the pretty fields and farmlands. I shook my head as I drove past Joyville Town Center, the Joyville Outlets, and the Joyville Shoppy Shoppes.

"You're killing me, malls," I muttered as I drove past.

As soon as I got home, I flopped on my couch and covered my eyes, trying to forget about today's disastrous practice. I grabbed Philly, a stuffed elephant my dad gave me. Philly always made me feel better. My cell phone started ringing. I groaned, but then I felt a little better when I saw who was calling. My mom.

"Hi, Mom," I said.

"Hi, sweet girl! How did your first practice go?" she chirped excitedly. My heart warmed. Leave it to my mom to be thoughtful enough to remember that practice started today. She totally ignored the fact that my coaching was a punishment to save me from jail. She acted like it was some kind of wonderful opportunity for me.

"It was..." Exhausting? Crazy? Full of simple-minded kids who had a better chance of being kidnapped by aliens than winning a baseball game? I found myself fantasizing about an alien ship coming down and abducting all my players and transporting them to a faraway planet. Konnie Mack can't serve out her sentence, the Judge Mann would have to say. Her whole team lives on Venus now. She's free to go. "Okay. It was okay, I guess."

"Well, good. I'm so happy you're finally getting back to baseball. I know how much it means to you," Mom told me. She really was a sweetie. She didn't have the passion for baseball that Dad had, but she really tried to take an interest in it for my sake. She'd never missed a single game I played in when I was a kid. She still didn't know much about the sport, but she wasn't anywhere near as bad as the kids on my team. She still called baseball scores "points" instead of runs, though. That's okay. It was kinda cute.

"I guess. It's not exactly how I pictured my return to baseball, though."

"I was afraid you'd never go back. I'm glad you did. It's good for you. You're so good at it, Konnie. The field is where you belong," Mom said, sounding happy for me. She used to love it when my dad would take me to ballgames. After he died, she told me how much it meant to him to spend that special time with me. I was both happy and sad thinking about that.

Of course, I was plain furious when I thought about that

last year when we were cheated out of that time together. The first year there was no baseball in Joyville and the last year my dad was still alive.

Yeah, well. Wait until she saw my team. She probably wouldn't be so happy when she saw us lose every game. Oh, well. Who cared if we won? All I had to do was get through the summer.

"I can't wait to see you play!" she said.

Well, my mom cared if we won. She wanted to see me do well. Though I didn't want to disappoint her, I wasn't a miracle worker. Not even the best baseball manager on the planet could get a win from these kids. And I was nowhere near the best manager on the planet.

In fact, I just might be the worst.

5

Thunk! I plopped my baseball equipment down on the Johnny Bench. *Pop*! I popped my gum, trying to get myself prepared for another practice. I was planning to make this practice short and sweet, with the emphasis on short. My punishment stated I had to hold practice twice a week, but nobody said how long the practices had to be. I'd be in and out of here in ten minutes if I thought I could get away with it. Maybe the kids wouldn't notice.

"Miss Konnie," grunted a deep voice.

"BAH!" The guy scared the balls and strikes out of me. With that voice, I half expected to see Catfish or Carl. Instead, it was the maintenance guy. He sure lived up to his nickname, The Giant.

"Sorry," he said, shrugging. "Didn't mean to scare ya. These boxes came for you." He plopped two big boxes onto the bench.

"Oh, cool. These must be the uniforms. Thanks!"

The Giant nodded shyly. He was a nice guy. A little bizzarro, but nice.

I looked out on the field to see that most of the kids had arrived. Joltin' Joanna was turning cartwheels in the outfield. George was munching on some chocolate chip cookies while Carl proudly watched. I wondered where a kid Carl's age had learned to bake. I hoped he brought enough for the whole team. Never mind that; I hoped he brought enough for me.

"All right, guys. Come on over."

The kids rushed over to me, eyes bright. Their enthusiasm was cute, if completely misguided. Odds were the other teams were going to beat the stuffing out of them, so what were they so happy about?

"Looks like our new uniforms came in," I told them. Squeals of excitement rose up from the crowd of kids.

"Oh, cool. Lemme see, lemme see!" Joltin' Joanna said, hopping back and forth from foot to foot.

"Whoooooa!" Catfish exclaimed as I opened the box.

Whoa was right. Holy home runs, I needed sunglasses to look at these uniforms. The colors were so loud they practically hurt my ears as well as my eyes. I supposed I shouldn't have been surprised. After all, the Joyville Sweat Sox were sponsored by Dizzy Dean's Paint Supply, whose motto was "Colors so Bright, They'll Make You Dizzy!" I guess old Dizzy wanted to show off his paint shades, because each uniform was a different color. Weird.

"Ooooh, they're so pretty!" Brooke said, as I pulled the jerseys out of the box. We had pink, blue, red, yellow, purple, orange, green, black, and white jerseys. I knew Brooke would want the pink one. I thought I had laid all the uniforms out on the bench, but there was one left in the box.

"Oh for the love of... They can't be serious with this!" I

yelled as I pulled out a large rainbow-striped jersey. The coach's jersey. My jersey. Oh, ick.

"I love it!" Brooke said, running her fingers over it admiringly. *You would!* I wanted to shout. I wanted to look like a strong, tough baseball coach, not a float in the Rose Parade.

"All right, let's figure out who's gonna wear what." I picked up the pink jersey first, which was bound to be the easiest one to figure out. "Who wants this one?"

I looked at Brooke. So did everyone else.

"Don't look at me. I'm not wearing that. What do I look like, some kind of girl?" She asked, earrings swinging and bracelets jangling. The hot pink jersey would have matched her lipstick perfectly. "I don't want pink."

"Fine. Who wants it?" I looked at Christy. Today she was wearing braids, which swung around and smacked her face when she shook her head. I looked at Joltin' Joanna.

"Get real," Joanna said.

The only other girl on the team was Ty. I knew better than to even suggest pink to her.

"Okay, fine. We'll put all the colors on a slip of paper and you can each pick one." I scribbled down the colors and mixed them up in my baseball cap. I offered the cap to Brooke, and she chose a color. I kinda hoped she would get pink after all.

"Purple!" Brooke said, looking pleased.

Yoyo chose next. He whispered his color, but nobody could hear him.

"Blue," I announced as I read the slip.

Joanna got yellow. I could just picture the blur of yellow as she turned cartwheels out on the field. Ty got red, which I thought was totally appropriate since she looked mad as fire all the time. Carl got orange, and Christy got green. Little Clueless got black, which was perfect because he always wore those dark, black knee socks. George got white.

Great, I thought. All those brownie and cookie stains would be highly visible on his uniform. Catfish was the last to choose.

"No," he said defiantly.

"No, what?" I asked him.

"No way. No way!" Catfish said, folding his arms. It took me a minute to figure out the problem. There was only one color left. *Pop*! This time I popped my gum to keep from laughing.

"Fair is fair, Catfish," I practically sang. He grabbed the last slip, which had the word PINK written on it in big letters.

Catfish crumpled it up and tossed it back in the hat. He looked so disgusted that I felt a sudden, surprising stab of sympathy for him.

"Catfish," I told him sternly. "This is your uniform. You wear it proud."

He looked up at me dejectedly. "Yes, coach."

I clapped my hands. "All right, guys. Let's get out there and practice!" The kids all whooped it up, clapping and dashing onto the field. I couldn't help but enjoy their enthusiasm. As I stood on the field, ready to address my team, I heard a car door slam. I looked up to see who it was. I noticed Ty looked up, too. She scanned the parking lot with a hopeful look on her face. She stared at the man walking toward the field, probably hoping it was her dad.

It wasn't.

Her face fell and she hung her head. I had a sudden urge to go over and hug her. Where did that come from?

"Well, well, well! Look at what we have here!" Gabe Steinbrenner said as he approached the field. *Pop*! I snapped my gum, waiting for an explanation as to why he was interrupting my practice. "Don't mind me. Just came to check out how my team is doing. You guys look great!"

I looked over at my team. They really did look nice all dressed up in their uniforms, gloves in hand and ready to go. Well, except for Joanna, who was wearing the glove on her head like a hat. Yeah, the team looked great to Gabe. That was because he hadn't seen them play.

"You guys ready to win some ball games?" he asked.

Oh, yeah. He definitely hadn't seen them play.

The kids cheered and shouted "YEAH!" Had *they* seen themselves play?

"Pretend I'm not here. Go on with your practice!" He gestured to me, then shouted, "Wee Willy! Get over here!"

A young man sprinted over. He was Wee Willy Martin, the man with the honor of having what was probably the worst job in town—Mr. Steinbrenner's assistant.

"Yessir!" Wee Willy said. He was a little younger than me. Fairly handsome, I guess. Brown hair, friendly brown eyes. He wore jeans and a T-shirt and looked a lot more laid-back than Gabe, who was always wearing those stuffy suits. He was calm and seemed to have a lot of patience. I guess you'd have to if you worked for Gabe.

"Sit here and watch the practice with me," Gabe said, taking a seat on the Johnny Bench. Wee Willy sat next to him like an obedient golden retriever. I half expected Gabe to give him a doggie treat for being such a good boy.

"Okay, okay," I said, trying to pretend Gabe and Wee Willy weren't there. "I think it's best that we start with the basics. Who knows what an 'out' is?"

Carl scratched his head. "Like out in the outfield?"

"Out in as in outer space?" Brooke asked, giggling.

"Hey," I said irritably. "Respect the game."

Brooke stopped giggling. Good. *Pop*!

"No, an 'out' is the way you kind of get rid of the other team so you can have a chance to bat. Like when other teams come here to..." I took a deep breath before I actually said it out loud. "...to L.O.S.E.R. Field, they are the visiting team so they come up to bat first. We have to get them out three times before we can have a turn to bat."

"Oh, yeah!" Christy said. "Like as in 'four strikes and you're out'!"

Pop!

"Three, Christy. Three strikes and you're out. But yes, you're right. That's one way to get an out. If a batter swings three times..." I picked up a bat, figuring a visual aid would help some of these baseball rules get through their heads. I swung the bat in the air "One! Two! Three! If the guy—or girl—swings three times and doesn't hit the ball, then they're out."

"Right, right, got it," Clueless said, nodding. "'It's one, two, three strikes you're out at the old ballgame.'"

"Exactly! Like the song!"

"What?" Clueless asked.

"Never mind," I said. "Okay, who knows another way to get a player out?"

"You can tackle 'em and make them fumble the ball!" Joltin' Joanna yelled out.

Pop! "No. That's football." I snuck a glance over at Gabe and was pleased to see that his brow was furrowed with worry. Good. I wanted him to see firsthand that winning with these guys was impossible, but it wasn't my fault.

"There are ways to get a batter out even if he hits the ball," I informed the kids.

"No way!" Catfish said. "If he hits it, it's a home run! Game over!"

There were so many things wrong with that sentence I didn't even know where to begin.

"Umm no. Not exactly. Not at all, actually. If the player hits the ball..." I tossed the ball into the air and smacked it with the bat. *Thwack*!

"WOW!" Brooke shouted and the other kids looked at me in such amazement that I chuckled out loud. It was so funny that they were excited I could hit a ball I had tossed to myself.

"If the batter hits the ball, she's gotta run to first base." I dropped the bat and ran to first base.

"WOW!" Brooke said again, apparently amazed at the fact that I could run to a base without messing it up. Holy home runs, were these kids easily impressed. It was kinda nice, though. It had been a long time since anyone was impressed by me. I was usually just getting in trouble for being mad.

"So, when you hit the ball, you run to first base as quick as you can and then step on the base. Then you're safe."

"Safe from what?" George asked, looking around nervously.

"Safe meaning you're not out. Now, if someone wanted to get you out—"

"Why would anybody want to do that?" Joanna asked, looking around suspiciously at her teammates.

"Because that's how you play the game. When the other team is up to bat, you want to get them out."

"I get it. When the other team is up to bat, we try to get them out. Three times. And then when we get up to bat, they will try to get us out three times so they can have a turn at bat again," Clueless Joe piped up. I just stared at him in wonder.

"Yes. Yes! That's it! That's exactly right!" I wanted to pick up little Clueless, perch him on my shoulders, and parade him around the field. Finally, somebody understood what I was saying! "So, getting a batter to swing three times and not hit the ball is one way to get an out. If the kid hits the ball, you can still get him out. All you have to do is to hurry up and get the ball to first base before the runner can tag the base."

The kids looked at me like I was trying to explain nuclear physics to them. I knew I was gonna have to take them through it step by step. I took a deep breath and chewed my gum.

Pop!

"Okay, let me show you." I tossed the ball up in the air and I hit it. This time I ignored their ridiculous cheers and shouts of congratulations because I had hit the ball. "Now pretend I'm on the other team!" I shouted as I ran for the ball, which had landed in the infield. I picked it up and dashed toward first base. "I hurry to get the ball and I have it with me when I step on first base. If I can get to first base—with the ball—before the runner gets there, then he's out."

"But," George began, looking worried, "what if the ball lands way out there? You know, where I'll be standing," he asked, gesturing toward center field. "How can I ever get the ball all the way to first base before the running guy gets there?"

"Good question!" I shouted, much louder than I meant to. George blinked, startled, then smiled. I couldn't help but be excited. It *was* a good question. It showed he'd been paying attention and had at least some idea of what I was talking about. "That's why we have a first baseman," I said, nodding at Ty. Ty punched her glove with her hand. Man, she could look pretty scary when she wanted to. "Whoever gets to the ball first, wherever you might be on the field, should throw it over to Ty. Ty will step on the base and get the runner out."

Ty nodded confidently and punched her glove again.

"Okay, let's practice. Pretend the batter just hit the ball," I said as I tossed the ball into the infield. "Now get the runner out!"

The kids all just stood there. *Pop*! *Pop*! *Pop*! "Somebody get the ball and throw it to Ty at first base!"

With that, all the kids except Ty went dashing for the ball. They ended up crashing into each other and collapsing onto the field. They just lay there like soldiers wounded on a battlefield.

I took a deep breath, fearing no amount of bubble gum was going to keep me from jumping up and down and screaming at this heaping pile of kids littering up my field. No one was more surprised than me at the words that came out of my mouth.

"Okay, guys. Good try, good try. Maybe I should have been more specific." Maybe I should have said *don't* go slamming into each other and knocking each other unconscious. "I should have said whoever is closest to the ball should grab it and throw it to Ty at first base to get the out. If it's close enough to Ty, she can just nab it and step on the base. If it lands close to George, George can pick it up and throw it to Ty. If it lands closest to Christy, then Christy can pick it up and throw it to Ty." So help me, I went through each and every player's name and explained that if it landed close to him or her, then he or she should throw it to Ty at first. I was slowly realizing there was no such thing as too much information when it came to these people. I practiced throwing the ball to each kid and let them each have a chance to get me out at first. After about a hundred billion tries, they started to get it.

"Okay," I said wearily. "Let's go over one other way you can get a runner out." I looked out at all the kids staring up at me expectantly, excitedly. I had to hand it to them. After a long practice with a lot of running around, they still seemed excited and eager to learn. Good for them. "If the batter hits the ball and you can catch it in the air, the runner's out."

"Really?" Catfish asked. "Cool!"

I smiled at him. "Yeah, I guess it is kinda cool."

"So you catch it and then throw to first base, right?" Brooke asked uncertainly. I was about to explain, but Clueless intervened.

"No, you don't have to. If you catch it like this..." Clueless tossed the ball up into the air and then caught it in his glove. "...and it doesn't touch the ground, you don't even have to throw to first. The batter's already out just 'cause you caught it. Is that right, coach?" Clueless looked up at me and I had the sudden urge to pinch his adorable little freckled cheeks.

"That's right! Exactly!"

Clueless smiled at me. For a kid named Clueless, he sure picked up on things quick.

"Hey, coach?" he asked.

"Yeah?"

"You're a good coach. You're nice. I'm glad they picked you to be our coach."

I looked down at him and then up at the other kids, who were all smiling and nodding. So they didn't know. They had no idea I was only here because it was my only choice besides going to prison. I looked up at Gabe Steinbrenner who arched an eyebrow and smiled slyly at me. I suppose it was a good thing the kids didn't know. Let them think I was coaching out of the goodness of my heart.

"I'm glad you're our coach, too," Ty said. She said it in

her usual tough voice and she didn't smile, but I'd take what I could get from that kid.

"Ummm, thanks. Thanks, guys." It felt good to hear that they liked me, but I did feel a little guilty that they all thought I was so great when I was technically a criminal.

Yoyo whispered something. I think. It's hard to tell when he's talking cause he's so darn quiet.

"What?" I asked.

Catfish rolled his eyes and then leaned down to try to hear what Yoyo said. Catfish brightened suddenly.

"Oh, yeah! When do we get our baseball cards?" Catfish asked.

"What are you talking about?" I asked.

"You know. Baseball cards. Like cards with our picture on 'em and stuff," he said.

I just stared at him."Are you serious?"

Nine heads nodded at me. Baseball cards. Really? Who did they think they were? Major leaguers? They barely knew what a baseball was. "No baseball cards," I told them. "That's crazy!" They all looked disappointed. I was surprised to find I felt a little bad. They were sweet kids. Still, the idea of doing baseball cards for these kids was nuts. I was required to coach them and that was it. I didn't have the time or the energy to make baseball cards for them.

"All right, guys. That's enough for today," I said, really meaning I'd had enough for one day. I gathered up the baseballs from the field and headed back to the dugout where Gabe and Wee Willy were sitting.

"So!" Gabe said brightly. "Are we ready to win some ball games?"

Both Wee Willy and I stared at him.

"You were here for the practice, were you not? I mean, you see what I'm working with here," I said, jerking a thumb toward the field where Joanna was turning cartwheels and Carl was trying, unsuccessfully, to juggle one baseball. It kept hitting him in the head.

"Well, yes..." Gabe said uncertainly. "But I'm sure you'll be able to work with them. You're the best, Konnie. I believe in you!"

"I don't know..." Wee Willy Martin said. "I mean, I'm sure you're good, Konnie. But you're not a miracle worker."

"Who asked you?" Gabe roared suddenly. "You know what? You're fired!"

I gasped, but Wee Willy didn't seem too upset.

"Okay, sir," Wee Willy said, standing up slowly. He headed out to his car with Gabe glaring after him.

"Look, Konnie," Gabe said to me. "It's vital that I have a good team. My reputation is on the line, here. I don't want to look like an idiot."

Too late! I wanted to shout. I popped my gum instead.

"It's very, very important that we win some ball games. Especially the games against the Cranksville Crankees." I could see the fire in his eyes. He really hated Bobby Hearsay. Not that I blamed him. I was no fan of his, either. After all, he was the jerk that stole baseball from Joyville. Still, Cranksville had been playing baseball for years, and I was sure they had a great team. Joyville had just gotten our team back and it was full of sweet but very inexperienced kids. Like Wee Willy said, I wasn't a miracle worker. "I want you to beat him and beat him good!"

The only chance I had at beating Hearsay at baseball was if I used a bat and whacked him in the stomach with it. Which was a rather tempting idea.

"Mr. Steinbrenner, with all due respect—" I began, gesturing over at my kids.

"I know, I know! I can see how tough it's going to be, but

you can do it. You have to! If for no other reason than to wipe that smug look off Bobby's face," Gabe said bitterly. "You ever meet the guy?" I shook my head. "You should. If you met him, you'd wanna beat him as bad I do." He sighed wearily and looked kinda sad.

Oh, did I mention Bobby wound up marrying that girl he stole from Gabe? Gabe really did have good reason to hate Bobby.

"I better get going. I'm starved. I'm gonna get Wee Willy to get me some..." Gabe glanced over where his former assistant had departed. "Oh, yeah. I fired him. I better call him and rehire him so he can get my dinner. See you later, Konnie! I know you can do it!"

I shook my head, laughing softly. The old man was out of his mind. We were definitely gonna get beat by the Cranksville Crankees and everybody else. The only question was—how bad would we lose?

I couldn't help but be curious about Bobby Hearsay, though. Maybe it was time I paid a visit to Cranksville.

6

Holy home runs. I could not get over the size of the Cranksville stadium. It was unbelievable. We had a field, but they had an actual stadium. It was called WIN! Stadium, because it was sponsored by the local WIN! Casino in Cranksville. They had actual permanent concession stands like they have in major-league stadiums. Not at all like the little hot dog and ice cream carts we had at our games.

It was easy to see where the team got all their money. *Everything* was sponsored by a company. The parking lot was called Whitey Ford's Ford Dealership Parking Lot. The dugout had a sign on it that said Rickey Branch's Tree Removal Service. There was a flag stuck in the middle of the grass that said Ozzie Smith's Lawncare Service: So Good You'll Flip!

The kids were out on the field practicing. They looked amazing, too. Their uniforms were actually *uniform* in that they all looked the same. You know, the way uniforms were supposed to. They were all dressed in black-and-white pinstripes that looked like prison uniforms. After all, the

Cranksville Crankees were sponsored by Barry Bond's Bail Bonds. The kids looked so sleek, so professional. Not at all like the Joyville Sweat Sox with all the crazy colors.

They also looked like they knew what the heck they were doing. They were good at everything. Each kid who came up to bat hit the ball hard, and I watched as the fielders quickly, expertly fired the ball to first to get the out. The balls that popped up high were caught effortlessly in the field.

Wow. Just wow. For a brief moment, I couldn't help but fantasize about what it would be like to coach this team instead. I quickly realized how disloyal that was. Joyville was my beloved hometown, and I knew I should be honored to coach their team. I couldn't help but think my dad would have been really excited to see me back on a Joyville team, even if we were horrible. I knew I'd never coach for a Cranksville team, or any team but Joyville. I really would choose jail instead.

"Well, well, well! Look who decided to pay us a visit!"

Bobby Hearsay strutted toward me. I wondered how he knew who I was. *Pop*! Went my gum. I could see what Mr. Steinbrenner had meant about Bobby's smug smile. He had that look on his face that meant he thought he was smarter and better than everybody else. He had grayish hair and he was dressed in a fancy, expensive suit, sorta like Mr. Steinbrenner wears. It was fine for Gabe to wear a suit, but Bobby looked like an idiot wearing one on the field. He was not only the owner of most of the town of Cranksville, but he was also the coach of the Crankees. He really should have been in the same uniform as his team. Instead, he looked more like a snobby bank manager. He looked down his nose at me just the way The Judge Mann did, except he looked really dumb doing it because he didn't even wear glasses.

"I'm Konnie Mack," I said, just in case he didn't know who I was.

He chuckled. Even his laugh was snobby. Like he was saying *heh heh heh, I'm so much better than you and you know it.* Bleh. "I know who you are," he said, winking. "I read the newspapers."

I already didn't like this guy. Jerk. I wasn't exactly fond of him before, and now that I'd met him, I really really really didn't like him. Double jerk.

"Great bunch of kids I got here, eh?" he said, gesturing with his head toward the field where the players were still chasing down the ball with expert precision.

"Yeah. They do look great out there," I grudgingly admitted.

"But then, you've got quite a crew yourself from what I hear," he said, nudging me and laughing. "A bunch of girls, some guys, and a...um...portly little fellow," Bobby opened his arms wide to indicate George's size.

Sudden anger rose up in me. My chest tightened and my fists curled. I'm always mad, so that didn't surprise me. What did surprise me was how mad it made me to hear somebody talk about my team that way. Sure, they were a little nuts, but they meant well and they tried really hard.

"Yeah, they're a really terrific bunch of kids," I said, also surprised to find I really meant it. "How do you know so much about my kids? I've never seen you at any of my practices."

He winked at me again. "Oh, I have my ways. You got a great big tall kid on the team, don't you?"

"Yeah. Carl Repkin, Jr. He's a big dude, all right."

"Kinda makes me wonder. You wouldn't have any kids that are too old to be on the twelve-year-old team, would you?" Bobby asked.

"What? No way. I'd never cheat."

"Sure, sure. I believe you. You know, what with your criminal record and all," he said, winking and nudging me again.

I wanted to blacken that eye with a punch so hard that he'd never wink again. Sure, I had a criminal record. Because some of the Joyville laws were stupid. All I did was get mad sometimes. That was it. I'd never lie or cheat or steal, especially when it came to baseball. Rule #7. Respect the game of baseball. No way I'd ever cheat.

"Well, with kids like mine, I don't need to cheat," Bobby said proudly.

"Yeah, my kids are great, too," I said.

Bobby laughed. And winked again. "That's cute."

Now I wanted to blacken the other eye. Too bad we had no shot at winning any games, especially against Bobby. It sure would be fun to beat him.

"Got some shrimpy little things on your team, too. That prissy little girl and the little itty bitty dude with all the freckles," Bobby said, making a face. He must have been talking about Brooke and Clueless Joe.

"They may be little, but don't count them out. Brooke's got an amazing throwing arm and Clueless Joe's smart as a whip," I said. Bobby laughed loud and long, right in my face.

Thwap! Cranksville's catcher caught the ball that had been thrown incredibly hard by their pitcher. Wow. I couldn't imagine how any batter would be able to hit that. Well, so what? Catfish had an arm that was just as strong if not stronger. He was just a little wild. Okay, a lot wild. He couldn't hit the broad side of a scoreboard with that arm of his...

"That's nice you think your kids are good. Cute, real

cute. Don't worry. Nobody's taking your team seriously anyway. Not like they're a real team or anything."

I dug my nails into the palms of my hand as my anger rose higher and higher. It was getting to a dangerous level. A level that would land me in jail real quick. Man, I really wish we had a way to beat his team! But I knew it was hopeless to even try.

Pop! I tried snapping my gum. I tried taking several deep breaths. My head was spinning and I knew I was losing control. I felt like I couldn't stop myself from throwing a full-out tantrum right there on the field. I was perilously close to yelling and screaming and pulling out Bobby's hair, clump by clump. I couldn't get mad, if for no other reason than I'd have to face that horrible, smug smile as he watched me get carted off to jail. I bit my lip, hard, to keep from going nuts. He chuckled as he watched. I think he knew he was getting to me.

"Well, I guess it's nice for you to have a baseball team back in Joyville again," he said.

I calmed down a little. I took another deep breath and pictured L.O.S.E.R. field. Yes. It was good to have a team in my beloved hometown again. That ballfield was like my second home. I was at peace there. Just thinking about it made me feel better. I loved, loved, *loved* having a baseball team in Joyville again. I'd even momentarily forgotten it was Bobby Hearsay's fault that we'd been without one for so long.

Bobby laughed again and shook his head. "Wow, that must've been really sad for you when I took the team from Joyville in the middle of the night." He laughed again, winked, and said, "I know your dad was sad about it, too. Probably made him even sicker!"

A bolt of white-hot fury shot through me, stunning me

with its ferocity. Tears of pain and anger stung my eyes as I thought of my dad. I turned and walked away before Bobby could see me cry.

My team was gonna kick Bobby Hearsay's butt if it was the last thing any of us ever did.

7

I knew it was gonna be nearly impossible for the Joyville Sweat Sox to beat the Cranksville Crankees. I had a better chance of becoming the President. Of Mars. But still, I knew I had to try. For me. For Joyville.

For my dad.

I thought about his kind eyes and gentle spirit. He was so calm and so nice. Not at all like me. Really the only time he yelled was at baseball games. I loved seeing him get excited when Joyville scored a run. He'd jump out of his seat and yell and high-five me. I never felt closer to him than when we were out at the old ball game.

I arrived early to L.O.S.E.R. field because I always liked to have a little time to myself before the kids got there. It made me feel closer to my dad. Like he was still here with me.

This time, I guess I didn't get there early enough because there was already somebody there. I was a little annoyed. But then, I'm usually annoyed. My irritation faded a bit when I saw it was Ty, practicing all by herself.

I watched her for a few minutes as I leaned against the

dugout. She kept tossing the ball up in the air and hitting it. Wow. She was getting pretty good. Then she practiced running the bases. Hard. Like she was trying to beat the tag and score the winning run. She flipped her short hair out of her face as she wiped the sweat off her brow. Her pants were streaked with dirt and it was obvious she'd been there for a while already. I never realized how serious she was about baseball. As I watched her, I couldn't help but imagine I must have looked a lot like her at that age. Running the bases, hair flying, pushing myself so hard.

Ty gasped suddenly, startled, when she saw me standing there. Then she glared at me.

"What're you looking at?"

"You," I said bluntly. Ty didn't seem to have a comeback for that. "Lookin' pretty good out there."

"Thanks," she said, not smiling.

I walked toward her. "You been practicing much?"

"Every single day," she said.

"Why?" I asked her. "I mean, that's good. I'm glad you're doing it and all. It's certainly paying off. But, you know, why?"

"I want to get good. I want to get real good in case my dad comes to a game." Her eyes were sorrowful, but her jaw was set with determination. My chest tightened with anger, but not at her. I hated that her dad made her so sad.

"You think he'll actually show up?"

Ty shrugged. "I hope so. Maybe. He goes to all my twin brother's games." She sighed deeply. "And all his practices. He plays football and I guess my dad likes that better. Maybe he likes my brother better."

"Oh, Ty. I can't imagine that's true. I'm sure it's not." *Maybe your dad's just a big fat jerk.* That was what I wanted to say. Ty didn't look convinced, and I wished there was something I could do to make her feel better. "Go to the plate," I instructed. She did, and I threw the ball to her. She hit a weak ground ball to the infield. "Not bad. Not bad at all!"

"It was pathetic. I didn't hit it hard enough."

"But you hit it. That's more than most of your teammates can do!"

Ty actually chuckled softly. "Good point."

I felt better that I had coaxed a smile out of her. She always looked so mad, but I guess deep down she was a good kid. She was a lot like me, I supposed. I tossed her a few more balls and she hit each one harder than the last.

"Excellent! Great job!" I told her after each hit. One by one, the other kids started to arrive. They stood around, looking impressed with Ty's hitting. I think it did them good to see one of their teammates doing so well. Who knows? Maybe we had a shot at beating Cranksville after all.

"All right, guys. Come on over. Whadya got, Carl?"

He grinned. "Cupcakes!" he said, smiling broadly. I couldn't help but smile back. I wondered if he'd grow up to be a chef someday. He did make some delicious baked goods.

"They're great!" George said happily, his mouth already full as usual.

"Let's go over what we learned at the last practice, okay? How many outs does the other team get before it's our turn to bat?"

"Three!" came the enthusiastic shouts of the kids.

"Great! There's a bunch of ways to get outs. Somebody tell me one."

Joltin' Joanna raised her hand and jumped up and down. "Oooh! Oooh!"

"Yes, dear," I said.

"You can get an out if you catch the ball in the air and it

doesn't hit the ground. Then the guy at bat is out out OUT!!!" Joanna said, and then turned three cartwheels.

"Very good!! And what's another way to get an out?"

Yoyo whispered something. Catfish rolled his eyes and then leaned down to listen. "He says you can get the guy out if you pick up the ball and throw it somewhere," Catfish translated for him.

"You pick up the ball and throw it to who?" I asked.

"Who's on first!" Catfish.

"I don't know who's on first. Depends on the team!" Joanna said.

"Well, yes I suppose…" I said. "The point is, you pick up the ball that's hit and you throw it where?" I snapped my finger and pointed at Clueless, figuring he would know.

"Do you want me to speak?" Clueless Joe asked.

"When I'm pointing at you, yeah," I said.

"You pick up the ball the batter hit and you throw it to the first baseman!" He said proudly.

"Yes!" I said enthusiastically. "And the first baseman—or woman in this case," I said, smiling at Ty, "needs to catch it and step on the base before the runner gets there."

Ty snapped her head sharply as if to say *Yeah. I got this.*

"Okay. What's another way to get a batter out?"

"Strike 'im out!" Brooke said, swinging an imaginary bat in the air.

"Yes!" I said, feeling better by the minute. If these kids could get the basic rules down and if they had any actual talent, maybe we had a shot at winning. That's a lot of "ifs," but you never know. Baseball is an amazing game. Anything can happen.

"And how many strikes to get a batter out?" I asked. *Please don't say four, please don't say four…*

"Three!" came the chorus of kids. I pretended not to see

Yoyo hold up four fingers, then quickly switch to three when he heard the others.

"Excellent! Okay, now that we've talked about how to get the other team out, let's go over what to do when it's our turn at bat. Ty, can you help?"

Ty eagerly stepped up to the plate, suppressing a smile. She always tried to act so tough, but I knew she was excited to be chosen. I tossed the ball to her, and she hit it. Hard.

"First you hit the ball, then you run like mad!" I said. Ty took off running toward first base.

"Ooh, running. I love running!" Joanna said. Why did that not surprise me? She took a sip from her squeeze bottle, and then started hopping around eagerly. "I wanna run, I wanna run!"

"You'll get a chance. Okay, to recap...when you hit the ball..." I pointed to Clueless.

"You run really hard to get to first base before the other team can throw the ball and step on the base and get you out!" he said eagerly.

"Yes! And remember, just like it's three strikes and you're out for the other team, the same is true for you."

"Hey! No fair!" Catfish yelled. I shook my head.

"Ty, I want you to miss on purpose this time, okay?" She nodded. I pitched the ball to her and she swung through it without making contact. "Strike one!"

"Awww. Good try. Better luck next time," Brooke said kindly. I shook my head again. I didn't bother to remind her that I told Ty to miss on purpose.

"Okay, here's a tough lesson about strikes. So hear it, learn it, deal with it, okay?"

They all leaned in to listen.

"You can get a strike without even swinging."

Gasps from all around. Yeah. I kinda figured that would blow their minds.

"If the pitcher pitches you a ball you really could have hit, it's called a strike. Picture an imaginary box from your chest to your knees. If the pitcher throws the ball in there and you don't swing, it's strike one on you."

Catfish shook his head. "Sooo unfair..."

"Welcome to the little leagues, soldier," I said. "If you see a pitch that looks good to hit, try to hit it. You got to keep in mind you can get three strikes without even swinging." The kids looked a little depressed at that idea. "But all is not lost, my little friends!" They looked hopeful. "You can also get to first base without even swinging."

"No!" shouted Catfish. "It can't be done!"

"But yes, my fishy friend. It can. If the pitcher throws the pitch into that imaginary box called the strike zone, it's a strike whether you hit it or not. But what do you think happens if he throws the pitch outside that box?"

The kids leaned in like I was about to reveal the mysteries of the universe.

"Then it's called a ball," I said.

"Isn't it always a ball?" Christy asked, braids swinging. She picked up the baseball. "A ball's a ball. Always. I mean, it's a ball, right?"

Pop! I wasn't really annoyed, though. I had expected this question. "Yes, it's still a baseball. But, if that baseball is pitched in the strike zone, it's called a strike. If it's pitched outside of the strike zone, it's called a ball. If you get three strikes, you're out. But what do you think happens when you get three balls?"

Their eyes widened.

"Nothing. Not one thing happens when you get three balls. BUT...when you get four balls...something magical happens..." I paused, dragging out the suspense. "If the pitcher throws four balls, then you get to strut right up to first base like you own the place."

"WHAT?" Catfish shouted. I actually giggled at his astonishment. He was too much sometimes.

"Yes! If you get four balls, it's called a walk 'cause you can walk right up to first base and *nobody* can call you out. They can't throw the ball to first to get you out or anything. You just get to go on first base. Totally cool beans, right?"

Eight kids nodded. Only Joanna frowned. "So you don't get to run?"

"Well, no..."

"That stinks! I'd rather stay at bat than just walk to first base," Joanna said.

Whatever.

"Okay, let's see...what else, what else...Oh, yeah. Foul balls!"

"Ooh! I know! I know! If you get a foul ball, then you have to go to the penalty box," Joanna said.

"Not quite. Well, not at all. No. There are no penalty boxes in baseball. A foul ball means you hit the ball..." I tossed the ball and hit it foul. "But it goes past those white lines. It just means it's out of bounds, and you kind of do a do-over. If you hit the ball foul, it counts as a strike against you."

"No fair!"

"Settle down, Catfish. Anyway, if you hit the ball out of bounds it's a strike, but it won't ever count as your third strike. The first two foul balls you hit are strikes, but you could sit there and hit foul balls all day after your second, and it won't be a strike. If you hit a ball foul, the other team can't throw the ball to first to get you out, but if they catch it without dropping it, you're out." I pointed at Clueless. "Recap that for us, would you?"

Clueless grinned. "Three strikes—yer out. Four balls—you walk to first and nobody can get you out no matter what. Hit the ball foul, it's a strike unless you already have two strikes. If you hit it foul, the other team can't throw you out at the base, but if they catch the ball without dropping it, then you're out."

I blinked at him. "Wow. You're all right, kid. You know that?"

Clueless grinned shyly. He just might have been the cutest kid I'd ever met. One of these days, I really would have to give in to the urge to pinch those little freckled cheeks.

"Okay, let's practice hitting. Brooke, let's start with you."

Brooke stepped up to the plate. Her earrings swung back and forth and her bracelets jangled as she held onto the bat. I stood behind her, helping her with her batting stance.

"Get a good grip on the bat. Back straight, elbows up. There you go. You look great!"

I walked to the pitcher's mound with a bucket of balls. I pitched one. She swung and missed. Badly. Forget strike zone—she didn't even seem to be in the right time zone. She practically swung before I released the ball.

"Okay, try again. Good try!" I pitched ball after ball after ball. After ball after ball after... Brooke still wasn't even close.

I went to the clubhouse and came back with a tee.

"Okay, let's practice with the tee, okay?"

Brooke nodded, smiling. To her credit, she didn't seem too upset that so far she was a complete and utter failure at batting. I placed the ball on the tee. She swung. And missed. Seriously, two-year-olds can hit off a tee! Brooke giggled.

"You're not respecting the game, Brooke. Respect the game," I said sharply. Brooke stopped smiling, and I felt a little bad. But still. She needed to take this more seriously if we were ever going to beat Bobby Hearsay's team.

Brooke tried again. And again. And again. I sighed heavily and went into the dugout. I emerged with a large, blown-up beach ball.

"Here!" I said irritably, as I perched the huge plastic beach ball on the tee. *If you can't hit this, then I'm gonna quit, I swear...* I popped my gum to keep from saying those words out loud.

Bop! She managed to make contact with the beach ball. The other kids cheered like Brooke had hit a game-winning home run.

"Good job," I said weakly. I didn't think I could take any more hitting practice, but they desperately needed it. "Ty, would you work with the team on hitting, please?"

She nodded, looking proud.

"Catfish, I wanna practice pitching with you," I said, lying. I wasn't any more excited about practicing pitching than hitting, but we had to do it. "Come on."

I left Ty to work with the other kids while I led Catfish around to the back of the dugout.

"Okay, here's what I want you to do," I said, drawing a circle on the back of the cement dugout wall with chalk. "Pitch the ball and try to get it in the circle. This way, we can work on your aim."

Catfish nodded, looking determined. He cocked his arm back and threw the ball impressively hard. Too bad he missed the circle. Too bad he missed the entire dugout wall, just like last time.

"Ow!" yelled Carl. I peeked out from behind the dugout wall to make sure he was okay. He was on the ground, rubbing his sore butt where the ball had hit him. He gave me a thumbs-up to show that he was okay.

I turned to face Catfish.

"Okay. Good try," I said. "Let's try again." I drew an even bigger circle. "Now try to hit this one."

Catfish cocked his arm back, looking determined. He missed the dugout wall just as badly as he had the first time.

"Okay, forget the circles. Just, you know...try to actually hit the wall..."

After what seemed like 90 hours and 500 million pitches, Catfish slowly got better at his aim. He had such a strong, powerful arm. If he could just control it, he would be unhittable. Another huge *if*.

Toward the end of what turned out to be a very long and tiring practice, I looked up to see some of the kids actually hitting the ball with Ty. And it wasn't the beach ball, either. I saw them hitting and practicing running to first. Catfish started actually hitting the dugout wall. He even started pitching the ball into the drawn circles, even if they were really big circles.

I felt a glimmer of hope. Maybe we really had a slim, teeny-tiny, itty-bitty, shot at winning a game after all. I guessed we would find out soon enough.

Our first game was on Saturday. Against the Cranksville Crankees.

8

I took a deep breath, taking in the wonderful sights and smells of the ballpark. The smell of roasted hot dogs, freshly mown grass, the smell of the dirt beneath my cleats. I was careful not to inhale too deeply when I stood next to Carl, though. I tried not to think of how many days it had been since he'd changed his underwear...

It'd had been a long time since I'd been in a ballpark on game day. It was exciting, but also a little scary. WIN! Field was pretty intimidating. The kids and I were used to L.O.S.E.R. Field, which was a lot smaller. I hoped the kids weren't too overwhelmed by the fancy schmancy-ness of the place.

George, for one, was having a grand time. There were more hot dog, pretzel, and ice cream stands than I could count, and I suspected he'd hit every one of them already. So far I'd just stopped by the soda stand, which was a weird experience. The guy selling soda, Murray Buttermaker, certainly said a lot of bad words for somebody who worked around kids. I'd gotten an earful when he accidentally dropped the first soda he'd poured for me.

I took my drink back with me to meet up with my kids and give them a little pep talk. I rolled my eyes as I looked at the doorknob on the clubhouse. *Chuck Knoblach's Doorknobs. Give us a turn!* I made sure I got them plenty of water and some stuff to snack on before the game.

"Here you go, guys," I said, handing out water bottles. "Drink up! I also got you some Moonlight graham crackers."

I had to admit, the kids looked pretty great all suited up in their uniforms. They were colorful, that was for sure, but it was kind of cool. I was kinda liking the idea that our uniforms were all different colors and that my rainbow coach's jersey had all their colors on it. Like I was representing each one of my little guys by wearing it.

The kids were chatting excitedly, tossing the ball back and forth and actually catching it. Except Catfish, who sat on the bench with his head in his hands.

"What's the matter, Catfish?" Man, I didn't think I'd ever get used to that name. I used to think Catfish must be a nickname. That was, until I met his brothers and sisters: Swordfish, Blowfish, Goldfish, and Starfish...

"I can't do this. I just can't. I mean, look at me!" he said, gesturing at his hot pink jersey. I felt kinda bad for him, but fair is fair. He chose the pink slip, so that was what he got.

"Catfish," I told him sternly. "That's your uniform. Be proud of it."

"Yes, coach..." he said glumly.

"No, I mean it. You get out there and you *rock* that jersey, you understand? I wanna see you strut out on that field like you own the place. You march out to that pitcher's mound and you *dare* people to make fun of you. Dare 'em with your eyes. You show 'em you're not ashamed and you ain't scared of nobody, you hear me?"

"Yes, coach," Catfish said, sitting up a little taller and sounding a little more self-assured. Wow. Maybe I wasn't a totally horrible coach after all. It was a good idea for him to look tough as a pitcher. In fact, we all needed to look pretty tough out there if we were going to have a shot at beating the Crankees.

What is this?" I asked, as I picked up a cute, cuddly, and non-tough-looking teddy bear.

"Oh, that's mine," Carl said. "That's Teddy Williams. I brought him for good luck!"

What, his dirty underwear wasn't enough of a good luck superstition?

"He can come with us out on the field so we'll be sure to win," Carl said enthusiastically.

Um, yeah. There was no way that was gonna happen. Look, we all got our good luck charms, okay? I've got Philly the Elephant, but you don't see him and his big old elephant snout on the field, now, do you?

"Um, that's great. But I think he'll be luckier if he stays in the clubhouse," I told Carl.

"But," Carl began, looking disappointed. "Well, okay." He patted Teddy Williams on the head and put him away. Little Teddy Williams looked kinda sad and lonely sitting in Carl's locker, but I really did not have time to worry about the feelings of a stuffed animal. We had a game to play —and win.

"Heyya, Coach? I got something for you. We can use it in today's game," George said, pulling something out of his locker. He handed me a baseball made entirely of wood. "I made it myself. We can use it as a good-luck charm."

"You...you made this?" I asked.

George nodded proudly. "Uh-huh."

I had to admire the craftsmanship. It was a perfectly rounded, smooth piece of wood. He had even etched in the stitches.

"I carved it out of a tree that got struck by lightning near my house. I named it Wonderball."

"You named it... I see. It's really cool, George. Nice job! But...I mean, we can't really use it in the actual game."

"Why not?" he asked.

"It's not regulation."

"Who's Reg Ulation?"

"I mean it's against the rules. Sorry," I said. It was cool-looking, but he didn't seriously think we could use it in the game. Did he?

"Oh," George said, looking dejected. He put the ball back in his locker.

I felt a little bad, but come on. A baseball made of wood? What next, a bat made out of vanilla pudding? The kids were starting to look a little down, so I figured I'd better say something to rally the troops.

"Are you guys ready to play some ball?" I asked, and was encouraged by the loud hoots and hollers from the kids. They looked and sounded like a real baseball team. Now it was time to put them to the test. "I know we can do this. Now let's get out there and win!"

"Yeah!" Clueless shouted. "All we need is four outs and then we'll have a chance to score some touchdowns!"

I just stared at him. Clueless giggled and then hitched up his black socks. "Just kidding, Coach. We got this."

I breathed out with relief. I was going to remind him about respecting the game, but I found myself laughing instead. I couldn't help it. He had me going there for a minute.

As always, the feel of stepping out onto that field took

my breath away. A slight breeze whipped through, stirring up the dirt around my feet. I closed my eyes and just breathed in the scent of the warm air, the grass, the dirt, the field. Oh, how I loved this game. How could I have stayed away so long?

The organist began to play the national anthem and a kid from Cranksville sang. Badly. Still, we all stood still and showed respect. The anthem ended and we applauded politely. As I walked over to Bobby Hearsay so we could exchange our team's lineup lists, I overheard some of the Crankees making fun of our uniforms.

"Holy cow! They look like a bunch of Skittles," said Phil Risotto, the Crankees' shortstop.

"I know, right?" said Cassie Stengel, one of the outfielders. "Next stop, the yellow brick road!"

With that, a bunch of the Crankees started singing "Somewhere Over the Rainbow."

Bobby Hearsay chuckled as he handed me his starting lineup. "Kids, huh?" he said. He sounded friendly, almost good-natured. Until he added, "Seriously, though. Your team looks ridiculous in those awful colors. Like a bunch of melted crayons."

I ripped the lineup card out of his hand and shoved mine into his chest.

"Whoa! Easy there, tiger. Wouldn't want you to get *mad* or anything!" He practically shouted the word "mad" as he looked around. He'd just love to get me in trouble for losing my temper. "All right, let's make this game short and sweet, shall we? I don't want my guys wasting their time and effort on your team," he practically spat out the words *your team.* "I mean, we have some real games coming up soon and I need them rested and ready."

"What is that supposed to mean?" I asked. *Pop*! I chewed

my gum really, really hard to keep from punching him in the gut.

"Oh, come on, Konnie. Your team's a joke. Everybody's been saying that. Even you've been saying it!"

Guilt twisted up in my stomach as I realized he was right. I had been whining about my team. Badmouthing the players I'd been stuck with. But as I looked at them out on the field now, I felt a little different. I knew how hard Clueless had worked to learn and explain the game to the others, how hard Ty had been working to push herself to be the best, how Catfish had thrown pitch after pitch after pitch until he got it right. Sure, Carl's underwear might stink and Joanna made herself dizzy in the outfield turning cartwheels and Brooke wore enough makeup to make a circus clown jealous, but they were good kids. Nobody was allowed to make fun of them but me.

"We'll just knock this game out real quick, okay? Don't worry. We have a mercy rule, so once we're ahead by twenty runs, we'll end the game," Bobby said, patting me on the head like I was a little kid. How dare he? How could he just assume he was gonna beat my kids by twenty runs? How could he assume he was gonna win at all?

Deep down, I was a little afraid he was right. After all, his kids were so good and my kids were, well...

Anyway, I realized there was nothing to be gained by standing here talking to Bobby anymore, so I simply walked away. I rolled my eyes when I saw that even home plate was sponsored by a company. It read *Big Bob Feller's Diner: Home of the Home Plate Special!!*

Brooke was up to bat first. She looked, well, *pretty,* in her purple jersey with her perfect makeup and earrings and other adornments. I couldn't help but cringe a little. I didn't want any of my players to look pretty. I wanted them to look rough and tough and scary. Like they were gonna be tough to beat. She might as well have walked out there with Teddy Williams under her arm.

The Crankees pitcher, Dodger Clemens, wound up and prepared to launch the first pitch of the game. I knew Brooke would strike out. I just hoped she wouldn't look totally ridiculous while doing it. I bit my lip.

Brooke was first-pitch swinging all the way. She took a huge cut at the ball.

And connected.

I gasped as I watched the ball go and go and go.

Holy home runs, Brooke Robinson just hit a home run on the first pitch!

Brooke stared at the ball and watched it sail over the fence. She frowned and said, "Oh, great. Now we'll never get the ball back!"

"Run, Brooke! Run the bases!" I screamed, and was proud of my ability not to add the words *You idiot!* after my instructions.

Brooke ran the bases joyfully and proudly stepped on home plate, smashing her foot down right on poor Big Bob Feller's face.

The crowd went wild. I went wild! The radio announcer, a guy named Mr. Spaulding whose head was big and round and resembled a huge baseball, went nuts.

"A HOME RUN! BROOKE ROBINSON OF THE JOYVILLE SWEAT SOX HAS HIT A HOME RUN ON THE FIRST PITCH!" shouted Mr. Spaulding.

The kids were all laughing and hugging and I knew it was a moment I'd never forget. I also knew I'd never forget the look on Bobby Hearsay's face as long as I lived. He just stood there, frozen.

Next up to bat was George. I knew it was crazy, but I

couldn't help but wish that another miracle would happen. Maybe he would hit a home run, too!

George stood at the plate. He tapped his bat on the plate like pro ballplayers do. He lifted up his finger and pointed directly at center field, as if gesturing that he was going to hit the ball out of the park. A shiver of excitement ran down my spine. That was, until George held up two fingers, and I realized he had been pointing at the Honus Wiener hot dog stand and was simply indicating that he wanted two hot dogs.

Then he struck out on three pitches.

Oh, well. He tried, I suppose.

The announcer went nuts. "HE STRUCK OUT! HE STRUCK OUT ON THREE PITCHES!" shouted Mr. Spaulding. Jeez, calm down already. I understood why he got all excited about the home run, but a strikeout? Really, dude?

I tried to ignore the fact that Joanna did cartwheels all the way up to the plate when it was her turn to bat. She struck out as well. Still, on the whole, I was pretty happy with the way the game was going so far.

While Clueless stepped up to bat, I went to the clubhouse to make sure Catfish was ready to make his pitching debut. He looked nervous, and I knew he was worried about wearing pink. I clapped him on the back and he stood up. I looked him in the eye.

"Remember what I told you, Catfish. You get out there and you *own* that pink jersey, you got it?"

He nodded. He took a deep breath. He ran his hand through his hair and looked me in the eye. "Yes, Coach."

After Clueless popped out, it was time for Catfish to make his appearance. He did exactly as I told him. He grabbed his glove and walked up to that mound with his head held high. The fierce glare in his eye warned everyone around him to think twice before mocking his jersey. To my astonishment, I didn't hear a single word from the Crankees about his uniform.

That's my boy, I thought proudly.

I hoped he would do okay pitching. He had such a strong arm, but his aim was still so wild sometimes.

He cocked his arm back.

I took a deep breath.

He launched the first pitch, which shot out of his hand like a rocket. The ball sailed past the Crankees batter and headed for the stands, sending all the fans screaming and ducking for cover.

"Ball one!" yelled the umpire.

No kidding.

"JUUUST A BIT OUTSIDE...OF THE BALLFIELD..." Mr. Spaulding informed everyone.

Catfish cocked his arm back for the next pitch. Everyone winced, ready to drop to the ground in case the ball headed their way instead of to the plate.

This time, Catfish's ball left his glove and headed straight for the Crankees dugout, sending the team scrambling and hiding under the bench.

"Ball two!"

Pop! It was so frustrating. Catfish had such a good pitching arm; he just had to learn how to control it and he'd strike everybody out. I couldn't help but be curious to see where his next pitch would land, though. I supposed it was too much to hope for that the next pitch would head straight for Bobby Hearsay's butt. That would totally be worth ball three...

Catfish wound up. People held up their hands, purses, or whatever they had on hand to protect themselves. Mothers shielded their children. Bobby Hearsay held up his clipboard in front of his face, leaving his butt totally unprotected...

Catfish's pitch shot past the plate, past the stands, and into the food vendor area. Murray Buttermaker let loose a string of bad words loud enough to make every parent in the stadium scramble to cover their kids' ears before they were scarred for life.

I knew I had to go to the mound to have a chat before Catfish killed us all. As the catcher, Yoyo came with me.

"If you pitch good, they will try to hit it," Yoyo whispered.

"Great. Very, very helpful, Yoyo," I said, rolling my eyes. "Look Catfish, you're doing okay!"

Catfish stared at me as if I had lost my mind.

"You're pitching hard, and that's good. Just keep your eye on Yoyo's glove, okay? That's where you're aiming the ball. If you pitch right to his glove, you're in the strike zone. You can do it. You hear me?"

Catfish smiled shyly and nodded. It felt good to see him show a little confidence. I couldn't believe how much good a few kind words could do. Who knew?

Yoyo put his mask back down and went back to his spot behind the plate. "He's gonna do good now. You better look out," he whispered to the batter.

"What?" the batter, Derek Cheater, asked, turning around to look at Yoyo. Just then, Catfish pitched the ball.

Thunk! The ball landed neatly in Yoyo's glove.

"Strike one!" said the umpire.

"HOLY COW! IT'S A STRIKE! I CAN'T BELIEVE IT! GAAAAH!" shouted Mr. Spaulding from the radio booth.

"No fair! He distracted me. He was talkin' to me!" Derek whined.

"No rules against talking," I murmured. It was a struggle not to yell it.

Derek grumbled, but couldn't really argue. Catfish wound up and pitched again. It was another spot-on pitch, right through the strike zone. Unfortunately, this time Derek was ready for it. He smacked the ball right to center field.

George was, um, you know...a little hefty, and I sincerely doubted he would make it to the ball in time, but he did. He did! He ran those crazy legs all the way to deep center field, settled under the ball and...and then some idiot in the stands reached out and caught the ball! George was right under it and had it all the way, but the fan interfered.

"FAN INTERFERENCE! FAN INTERFERENCE!" shouted both me and Mr. Spaulding. The umpire just shook his head.

"Nope. It was a home run. He hit it right out of the park and into the stands," the umpire said. He twirled his index finger around in a circle, meaning it was officially a home run. I wanted to bite that finger right off.

"That's not possible! The kid reached over and took it right out of George's hand!"

"No way. Sorry!" the umpire said cheerfully. On the sidelines, Bobby chuckled and I wanted to tackle him to the ground, like in a football game. I looked helplessly at Catfish, who shrugged his shoulders sadly. Over in center field, George looked equally dejected. It was so unfair, but there was absolutely nothing I could do. If I got mad or argued with the umpire, I'd be carted off to jail. I couldn't let that happen, especially not in front of my kids. They had no idea that I was only coaching them to avoid jail and I wanted to keep it that way. They were happy playing baseball with me and they didn't need to know the ugly truth.

I felt horrible. It was a terrible call, and now the score was tied.

Catfish struck out the next two batters, and I started to feel better. The next batter up, Osay Canuseeco, popped up the ball when he hit it. Christy was totally on it in the outfield. She caught the ball effortlessly. I was so proud! Ball firmly in her glove, she kept running backward until she crashed into the wall. Why would she keep running? She had the ball!

I asked her when she came back to the dugout.

"That's how the pro ballplayers do it! I seen 'em on TV. They always crash into the wall."

"Um, yes. Well, that's only when they're running to catch it. You don't to have crash into the wall if you've already caught it," I told her.

"Where's the fun in that?" Christy asked.

"Hey, we're not here for fun. Respect the game. We're here to win. You only crash when you have to."

"Yes, Coach," she said a little sadly.

"Okay!" I said, clapping my hands. "Next up to bat—Yoyo, Ty, Christy!"

As the kids got ready to bat, an ear-piercing scream came up from the crowd.

"YEAH! ALL RIGHT! LET'S GO!" shouted a woman in the stands.

"Who in the world is that?" I asked.

"Oh," Catfish replied. "That's Yoyo's Ma."

"You can't be serious!" I said. Yoyo, who spoke so softly you couldn't hear a word he said, apparently had a mother with a gigantic mouth.

"I know. Go figure, right?" Catfish said, chuckling.

I smiled at him. "You're doing great. You are rockin' that jersey, by the way."

He laughed again and smiled at me. "Thanks, Coach. I'm getting used to it, I guess."

"Go, Yoyo, go! Go, Yoyo, go!" shouted Yoyo's mother.

"Go, Yoyo, go!" I repeated. His mother smiled and gave me a thumbs-up.

Yoyo hit a soft grounder and made it to first base. The crowd went wild.

Ty was up next and hit a line drive. Base hit. Two runners on, nobody out. I glanced over at Bobby Hearsay, whose face was completely red. I giggled as I watched him break his clipboard in half over his knee.

Next up was Christy. She hit a ground ball that got past the first baseman, Jade Woggs. I couldn't believe how well this game was going. Jade picked up the ball at first base, but it was way too late to get an out. Still, she threw the ball to Arod Rodriguez at second base. I gasped as I saw the umpire hold up two fingers.

"DOUBLE PLAY!" shouted Mr. Spaulding.

Double lies! I wanted to shout.

"Christy was already on base when Jade got the ball and threw it to Arod. And he didn't even catch it! It hit him in the chest! No way are my guys out!" I shouted.

"Calm down, my dear," Bobby said casually. "So sorry, but the umpire's word is final. Isn't that right, James?"

The umpire, James Joyce, nodded and winked at Bobby. Bobby winked back.

Oh, no... It was so obvious to me now. The umpire was on Bobby's side. I didn't know if Bobby had paid him off or what, but he was definitely blowing the calls on purpose.

I felt awful. It was so unfair to my kids. They were

working hard to win. I didn't know what to do. I wasn't allowed to get mad.

Just like that, we had two outs instead of two runners on. Carl was up next. He stood in the batter's box. He was even taller than the umpire.

"Wait a minute! Wait a minute!" Bobby said, rushing over, pointing a bat in my face. The bat was sponsored by *Cool Poppa Bell's Popcorn: So Good You'll Go Batty!*

"What?" I asked through clenched teeth. I'd never hated anyone so much in my life.

"This boy," he said, gesturing at Carl, "is clearly too old to be on the twelve-year-old team."

The umpire took off his mask and eyed Carl suspiciously. I almost couldn't blame them for questioning Carl's age. I remember wondering the same thing when I first met him. But he *was* twelve.

"I'm afraid I'm gonna have to see his birth certificate."

"Fine," I said bitterly. "But it's not like I've got it in my back pocket right now. I'll get it to you later."

"Sorry! If you want him to play, I'm gonna have to see proof of his age. Now." Bobby said. The umpire nodded, of course. I sighed heavily.

"I'm sorry, Carl. You can't play until next game."

He nodded. "I understand, Coach," Carl said. He patted my arm, then glared at Bobby. I swallowed hard and called Joanna up to the plate.

She struck out. Or, should I say, she supposedly struck out. A lot of the pitches looked like balls to me, but of course the umpire didn't call them that way.

And so that was how the game went. Before I knew it, we were behind 21-1.

"I guess that's it," I said wearily to Bobby. The mercy rule. We were behind by twenty runs, so that meant the game was over. It was a rule designed to protect kids, especially ones who were just starting out and learning the game. Twenty runs was enough and it was considered the nice thing to do to end the game before they lost by any more.

I hated to admit defeat, but there was no beating this guy. You couldn't beat somebody who played dirty, and I wouldn't cheat no matter what. My dad raised me to love and respect baseball, and I would never, ever dishonor the game by cheating. Still, it was so unfair. To me, to my kids. I could barely keep the tears from welling up. So, so unfair.

"No way. I wanna keep playing!" Bobby said, an evil glint in his eye.

"You're ahead by twenty runs, Bobby," I said. Then, lowering my voice so only he could hear, I said, "Because you're a horrible, worthless cheat."

"I wanna keep going!" he insisted, no doubt wanting to win by more.

I sighed and then gathered my kids around. "Look," I said softly. "It's okay to stop now. They're ahead by twenty runs, so if we want, we can—"

"I want to keep playing!" Clueless said, hitching up his big, black socks.

"Me too," Ty said, a defiant look in her eyes. She was no quitter, that one. Judging from the nods from all the other kids, none of them were.

"Are you sure?" I asked. I was so worried about my little guys. I didn't want them getting hurt.

"Yeah," Catfish said. "We're not quitting just because the other team is cheating."

I hadn't realized that my kids had figured out what was going on. I was amazed. They knew what they were up against, and they still wanted to play on. I felt so inspired as I looked into their determined faces.

So we played on. And lost 36-1.

But we played fair and square. I couldn't have been prouder of my kids.

9

As I headed toward the dugout, I realized I had no idea of what to say to my kids after this awful game. Would they wonder why I hadn't stood up to Bobby? They had no way of knowing what would happen to me if I got into an argument. I hated for them to think I wouldn't stand up for them, but that was better than them finding out the truth. Their feelings would be really hurt if they knew I was only coaching them so I wouldn't go to jail.

Well, that was why I started coaching them. Things had kind of changed for me. I'd found I rather liked these kids.

As I reached the clubhouse, I overheard Gabe Steinbrenner firing Wee Willy Martin as his assistant again. Somehow, he figured Joyville's loss against the Crankees was his fault. This time, I knew better than to worry. Wee Willy would probably have his job back before they reached the car.

I walked inside the clubhouse and a delicious smell filled my nostrils. Carl was over in the corner, frying up some burgers.

"Are you frying? There's no frying! There's no frying in baseball!" I told him.

"I figured we could use a treat after such a tough loss," Carl said, wiping his hands on his apron. Yes, he was wearing an apron. He was so weird! But so sweet. Seriously, what a great kid.

"That's really nice, Carl. Really nice. Thanks, kiddo," I said, tousling his hair. Of course, I had to reach up on my tippy-toes to do it. He smiled at me and offered me a burger. It was delicious.

"Guys, seriously, I cannot even begin to tell you how proud I am of how you did today," I told them.

The kids looked very proud of themselves, which they should be. I even noticed a small smile cross Ty's lips. With a dad like hers, I'm sure she wasn't used to praise no matter how much she deserved it. Joanna took a sip of her squeeze bottle and started hopping around the clubhouse. I was really starting to wonder what was in that drink of hers.

"And I'm, you know, really really sorry that the Crankees did, you know, what they did..."

"You mean cheat," Catfish said. "They cheated. Like, a lot."

"Like, I know," I said, sighing. "And it was really unfair. But I'm so proud of the way you guys stuck it out. You lost, but you lost honestly. The only way you really lose is if you sink to their level. If we had cheated, we would have been the real losers."

The kids nodded, and my pride swelled again.

"Don't be so sad," Brooke told me. She walked over and lifted up my chin with her tiny, delicate fingers. "You know what will make you feel better? A makeover!"

"You cannot be serious," I said, making a face.

"Come on. Just 'cause you're like the sporty type doesn't

mean you can't be pretty, too!" Brooke informed me. If anyone else had told me that, I'd have popped my gum in their face and told them they were nuts, but Brooke? Brooke was living proof that you could wear makeup, jewelry, and look all fancy-pants and still hit a home run on the first pitch. Maybe she was right.

"Okay, maybe, *maybe* I will let you do a makeover on me, but first we have to wrap up here. We'll need clean uniforms for the next game, and I ain't your mama so I ain't doing your laundry. Rule #3: Everyone Will Take Turns Doing the Team's Laundry. Remember what I told you—a red tag in your locker means it's your turn to wash the team's clothes."

I watched as each kid got up to check their locker. Brooke took a deep breath and slowly opened her locker. She breathed out a huge sigh of relief when she saw no red tag. Carl simply shrugged when he opened his locker and found no tag. Yoyo jumped up and waved his arms—silently —when he saw it wasn't his turn. Christy very slowly, carefully opened her locker.

"NOOOOOOOOO!" she wailed when she saw the tag. Jeez, drama queen much? I rolled my eyes as I watched all the kids gather around to comfort her. These kids were just too much.

And I wouldn't trade them for anything in the world.

I LOOKED at myself in the clubhouse mirror as I mentally prepared for today's game.

Okay, I had to give Brooke credit. I don't usually wear a lot of makeup, but she'd done wonders with my face. I loved the look of the eyeliner she applied. It made my blue-green eyes really stand out. I also realized wearing a little light lipstick wouldn't kill me. She seemed delighted to see me looking more presentable, and making her happy was definitely a plus.

Yes, these kids were weird, but they were all mine.

I found I was really excited about today's game. I was hopeful it would be a *real* game, and not one where we were up against a bunch of jerks who refused to play fair.

The opposing team today was from the town of Boring.

Yes, Boring. I am not making that up. The team is the Boring Blu Rays, as they were sponsored by a company that made Blu Ray discs. They all wore, well, a boring shade of blue, which made me appreciate my colorful group all the more. At first, I'd been kind of ashamed of our uniforms, but now I could see they totally rocked.

I motioned for Catfish to come over.

"Yeah, Coach?"

"Guess what? I think you've got some fans out there today," I told him as I pointed to the stands. Sure enough, there was a group of giggling girls who were all wearing the same shade of hot pink as Catfish's jersey. They wore handmade shirts that had #29 on them. Catfish's number.

Catfish's eyes grew wide. "No way! And they're pretty, too! Look at 'em!"

I nodded and smiled.

"I have fans, Coach. Actual fans!"

"Of course you do. Why wouldn't you?" I loved seeing the excited look on his face. It was a far cry from how depressed he was when he first had to wear the jersey.

"Fans...I have fans...*girl* fans..." he mumbled as he walked away in a daze. I chuckled out loud. He was adorable. And happy. I loved seeing my kids happy.

As I headed over to give the other coach my lineup, I nearly tripped over something in the field. "What the—"

A goose. It was a goose. There was a goose standing there, blinking at me, in the middle of the field.

"Hey there! I see you've met Gossage!" came a cheery voice.

"I've met who?" I asked, looking up at the Blu Ray's coach.

"Gossage!" he said. "He's kinda like our honorary mascot. He hangs around the field. He spreads good luck and cheer for our team!"

"Oh. I see." I couldn't help but wonder what else the goose spread over the field and who was responsible for cleaning it up. I glanced over and saw The Giant emptying one of the stadium trashcans. Poor guy. I guess it would be up to him. He cleaned up pretty much all the baseball fields around here. He should get extra money for this one.

"I'm Stan Musical. It is so nice to meet you!" Stan said, offering his hand. He was a skinny guy with a moustache and a friendly smile. As I shook his hand, I felt an immediate sense of relief. Clearly, this game was going to be nothing like the last one. Stan seemed like a really cool, nice guy. Finally, my kids would have a chance to play a real game, fair and square. "What a great day for a game! Your kids look great, just great! Let's have some fun out there!"

"Sounds good to me," I said. Sheesh. This guy seemed a wee bit overeager. He'd get along well with Mr. Spaulding. And Joanna, for that matter. All three of them needed to calm down a bit, but I suppose I'd take their excitement over Bobby Hearsay's meanness any day.

"Hey, you've played against the Crankees before, right?" I asked. Stan's face fell for an instant. It was so quick I almost missed it, but I saw it. Then he brightened immediately.

"Why, sure I have! He's great! His team is great!" Stan said, but this time his enthusiasm was totally forced.

"Really," I said dryly. "Come on now, be honest."

"Why, whatever do you mean?" Stan asked. I swore his teeth were clenched.

"He cheats, Stan. He did it to my team and I'm sure he's done it to yours."

Stan finally dropped the nicey-nice act. "Okay, fine. Yeah, he's a big cheater. A big fat cheater. Sometimes I'd just like to take his face and shove—" He stopped suddenly, realizing what he was saying. "But, you know. What are you gonna do? Not everybody is a great sport like we are, eh?" he said, nudging me a little too hard.

"Ow! What do you mean, 'what are you gonna do?'" I said irritably. "I'll tell you what you should do. You should tell The Judge Mann what he's up to."

"Oh, no no no. I couldn't be a snitch. That wouldn't be nice," Stan said, looking worried. I wanted to give him more to worry about than being a snitch. He should worry about my fist connecting with his gut.

"Nice?" I said super-sweetly, trying my best not to kill him. "Why do you think it wouldn't be nice?" *Pop*!

"Oh, I just couldn't be a tattletale. That wouldn't be fair."

"You know what's not fair?" I said, struggling to keep my tone even and my hands from wrapping around his scrawny neck. "What's not fair is keeping honest, hardworking players like my kids from having a chance to win."

"Hmmm," he said. "I guess you have a point there. Well, have a great game out there, sport!" Stan said, punching me lightly in the shoulder. With that, he walked away humming "Take Me Out to the Ballgame."

I was crushed. For one brief moment I had hoped that maybe, just maybe, Stan would help me take Bobby Hearsay down. Cheaters like Bobby can only get away with stuff like that if nobody is willing to speak up about what they're doing. I would gladly speak out against Bobby, but with my criminal record, nobody would believe me. I could wind up in jail for getting angry with Bobby even though I had every right to be mad.

I sighed heavily and trudged back toward the dugout, almost tripping over that stupid goose again.

"Stan! Do you mind getting rid of your little mascot here?" I called over to him.

"Sorry. Can't do it. That wouldn't be nice. He loves baseball! He's great!"

I slowly turned around and headed back to the dugout. *Pop*! If Stan was so nice, how come I wanted to smack him on the back of the head?

"Hooooonk!" said the goose.

"Oh, shut up!" I told him. At least I could yell at Gossage and not get in trouble. I'd like to see him tell The Judge Mann I got mad.

Since we were the visiting team here at Boring Stadium, we were up to bat first. Brooke stood up at the plate. Since she'd hit it outta the park against the Crankees, I was eager to see how she would do against the Blu Rays.

The pitcher for the Blu Rays was a kid named R.A. Stickey. R.A. wound up and got ready to release the ball. Then nothing happened. Brooke looked at me and I shrugged. I looked back at the pitcher only to see the ball had somehow gotten stuck to his hand.

"Sorry," R.A. said. "My bubble gum got stuck on the ball."

Great. Stickey, indeed...

"That's all right, boy! That's all right! You're doin' great!" Stan yelled out. *Oh, yeah. The kid got the ball glued to his own hand but he's doing great.* The kid managed to get the ball unstuck. He wound up again, and this time he was actually able to pitch. The ball wobbled up and down in the air as it sailed to the plate. It hit Brooke on the shoe and bounced into the stands.

"Ball one!"

No kidding. At least we had an honest umpire this time.

The kid pitched again, and the ball wobbled up and down. Brooke took a swing at it and missed. She did it twice more and struck out.

"Good try, Brooke. Good try!" I shouted. I didn't want to be like Stan and tell my kids everything they did was *great*! but it really was a good try. Sure, she struck out, but she kept the bat straight and kept her eye on the ball. I was proud of her.

R.A. Stickey somehow managed to get two more batters out, despite getting the ball stuck to his cap, his elbow, and on the end of his nose. Regardless, Stan Musical told him he did *great*!

Catfish took the mound. He kept glancing out at the crowd, where his fans were squealing and chanting his name. I hoped he wouldn't get too distracted to pitch well. When he finally turned his attention back to the mound, he looked pretty focused. Good. The first two pitches he dealt were excellent. Right down the middle. The Blu Ray batter, Joe Smarter, just stood there, looking confused.

"I don't get it. I didn't even swing. How come I got two strikes?" he asked.

Stan just shrugged and said, "You're doing great!"

Seriously, could Stan be more useless? It is confusing that you can get strikes without swinging, but I explained that idea to my kids right away!

Joe finally swung at the next pitch and, to everyone's amazement, he actually hit the ball and ran to base.

Third base.

Joe Smarter ran to third base instead of to first. Unless his middle name was "Isn't," his name was a total lie. His whole team cheered him on.

"Great! Great job! You're doing great!" Stan yelled.

I stood there and waited for him to correct Joe and move him to first, but he didn't. Catfish and I just looked at each other. I held up a hand to him as if to say, *Don't worry. I got this.*

I walked over to Stan and cleared my throat. I cleared my throat again, louder, so as to be heard over his humming of "Take Me Out to the Ballgame."

"Uh, Stan? Your kid is on third base. He should be on first. You run the bases counterclockwise, ya know," I said, again proud of being able to resist adding *You idiot!* to my comment.

"I know that," he said.

"Well, then, would you mind telling him that?" I said, jerking a thumb over in Joe "*NOT*" Smarter's direction.

"Oh, I sure do hate to hurt his feelings. Couldn't we just let him have a triple?" Stan asked.

Pop!

"No," I said, my voice barely a whisper. "No, we can't. He needs to be on first." Was this guy insane? No, I was not about to award the kid two extra bases because he was too dumb to run them in order!

Stan grudgingly walked over to Joe to straighten him out. I couldn't help but notice that Stan pointed in my direction, no doubt telling his player that Mean Old Konnie Mack was making him go to first. Whatever.

"And now the triple has turned into a *single*!" shouted Mr. Spaulding from the announcer's booth.

"It was *never* a—" I began shouting over to Mr. Spaulding. "Oh, forget it."

"Aw, man," grumbled Joe Dumber. "I was this close to getting a field goal.

I sighed. I looked over at Stan, waiting for him to correct his player.

"You're doing great!" Stan told him instead, holding up a dorky thumbs-up. "Maybe next time!"

I just shook my head.

The next kid, Carlos Delgottago, held the bat upside down. I corrected the bat for him while Stan told him he was "great!" Catfish patiently waited until the batter was ready, and then he pitched the ball. Unfortunately, Carlos decided that would be the perfect time to bend down and tie his shoe. The ball bounced right off his butt.

"OW!" Carlos yelled, grabbing his little tush. I saw Catfish cover his smile with his glove. Good sport that he was, he jogged over to the plate to see if Carlos was okay.

"Ease his pain," Yoyo whispered through his catcher's mask.

"Eat his brain? What? Speak up, man!" Catfish yelled.

Stan looked worried about his player, but of course did not tell him the importance of paying attention to the ball in order to avoid being nailed in the bottom with it.

"You're doing great, Carlos," I told him before Stan could say it. "But you gotta make sure you keep your eye on the ball, okay? Don't want anybody getting hurt out there."

Carlos nodded and, to his credit, sucked it up and got ready to bat again. Sheesh. It was crazy how Stan refused to teach his kids anything about baseball for fear of hurting their feelings. Watching the Blu Rays play showed me what would have happened to my guys if I hadn't bothered to teach them anything. They'd still be looking for a net and trying to score some baskets.

Even though it was totally his fault because he had

leaned into the pitch when he got hit, I decided to be a good sport and let Carlos take first base. Next up was Candy Malomar. She managed to hit a long fly ball. For an awful second, I was afraid that it might have been a homer. Thankfully, Christy was under it and caught the ball for the out. Just then, someone in the stands reached out and snatched her baseball cap right off her head.

"What the—" asked Christy as she whirled around. I looked closer and saw it was the same bratty kid who had snatched the ball out of George's hand at the other game.

"GAHHHHH! I CAN'T BELIEVE IT! A FAN STOLE THE OUTFIELDER'S HAT! WHOAAAAA NELLIIIEEEE!" screamed Mr. Spaulding in the radio booth. Seriously, somebody needed to medicate that guy or something.

"You're gonna lose! You're gonna lose!" shouted the bratty kid.

"What is that guy's problem?" I asked.

"Oh, that's Jeffy Myers. He shows up to all the games and causes all sorts of trouble," Stan said. "He's great!"

I resisted smacking Stan on the back of the head, but it wasn't easy. "How can you say he's great?"

"Oh, I just feel bad for the guy. See, he's not allowed to play baseball anymore. He's been banned for life."

"Banned for life? Why?" I found myself feeling sorry for the little brat. I couldn't imagine being banned from baseball for life. That was a worse punishment than anything I could think of.

"He retransmitted without the express written consent of Major League Baseball," Stan said somberly.

"Oh. That would do it."

"Yep."

"Wow."

We went on with the game, but it didn't last much

longer. Joyville was ahead 20-0 by the second inning, so we called it quits due to the mercy rule.

"Now *that* was a real Boring game!" Stan said.

That game was a lot of things, but boring it wasn't. I tried not to listen as Stan told his team how *great*! they had been. *Please. Don't make me vomit*. If anyone had no respect for the game, it was Stan Musical.

I wearily packed up the equipment. For a two-inning game, it felt like it went on forever. As I put my baseball stuff in my car, I heard Joanna's scream all the way from the parking lot.

I guess she found the red tag.

10

As usual, I showed up early before the next game so I could have a few moments to myself on the field. And, as usual, my plans were foiled because some kids showed up early.

I couldn't help but smile. I was actually glad to see them. I waved to Ty and Brooke as they practiced tossing the ball to one another. The Giant was dusting off the bases while trying not to get drilled in the head with the baseball. He really did do a good job keeping the fields looking nice. At least here at Oreo Park at Nabisco Yards there didn't seem to be any geese or other animals wandering around the field. The Giant smiled and waved at me and I returned the gesture.

I went inside the visiting clubhouse where we would get ready to play the Balmer Oreos. Carl was in the clubhouse already, neatly ironing all of our uniforms.

"What are you up to, Carl?"

He looked up from the ironing board. "They don't call me Iron Man for nothing," Carl said, grinning.

"I thought it was Joanna's turn to do the laundry."

"It is, but you know. I don't mind."

"Here, let me help you," I told him as I took Yoyo's blue uniform and hung it up in his locker.

"Thanks!" Carl said.

I helped him finish up the uniforms, and then went back out to check on Ty and Brooke.

"Gotta get ready," shouted Brooke to Ty. "Be right back!" Brooke disappeared into the clubhouse. Ty stayed outside since she was already dressed in her red Joyville uniform.

I grabbed a baseball and Ty and I started tossing it back and forth.

"You're getting really good, you know? I can tell you've been practicing a lot."

"Thanks," Ty said quietly. She didn't look quite as angry as she used to. Her face looked softer but more weary. She blew the hair out of her face and then gazed over at the parking lot. "My dad said he would come today."

My heart broke for her. Sure he said he was coming. He always said he would come to her games. He never did.

"Do you think he'll show up?" Ty asked me hopefully.

"Do you think he will?"

"I don't know," Ty said. "I hope so."

"I hope so, too, Ty. But you know...try not to be sad if he doesn't, okay?" She nodded, but I knew she would be sad. She always was.

"I was really lucky, you know? My dad was great. He loved baseball as much as I do. Used to come to all my games. I know you're sad when your dad doesn't come see you. I would be, too."

"How come your dad doesn't come see your games now?" Ty asked as she tossed the ball to me.

I swallowed hard before answering. "He died when I was sixteen."

Ty fell silent after that.

Brooke came out of the clubhouse, dressed in her purple uniform. She'd also added her rings, bracelets, and necklace.

"You look nice," I told her.

"So do you. I'm loving the black eyeliner on you," she said proudly.

I laughed and said, "Me, too."

Brooke, Ty, and I tossed the ball around a bit more as the other team members started to arrive. Each kid went into the clubhouse to receive a freshly ironed uniform, courtesy of Carl.

"Okay, guys. Let's get ready to play some ball!"

The kids all lined up and stood at attention for the national anthem. They looked so confident, so ready, and oh-so-colorful. We all jumped, startled, when the crowd yelled "O" for Oreos when they got to the part about "Oh\ say does that Star-Spangled Banner yet wave." It made me wish there was a "J" in there somewhere so we could yell, too.

After the national anthem was done, the kids all ran off to start the game. Everybody, that was, except for Ty. She just stood there for a moment, looking up at me.

"Coach?" she said.

"Yeah?" I responded, shielding my eyes from the sun so I could see her.

"I'm really sorry your dad died."

Wow. Tears formed in my eyes. "Thank you, Ty. Me too."

She ran off to join the rest of the team. I looked over at my rainbow-colored lineup. Yeah. They were the best.

The game against the Balmer Oreos was uneventful, for the most part. We were tied 1-1 most of the time. Not the most exciting game, but you'd never know it by listening to Mr. Spaulding's radio announcing.

"HE FOULED OFF THE BALL! WOW! LOOK AT THAT!"

"AND WE GO TO THE THIRD INNING STILL TIED. CAN YOU BELIEVE IT?"

"WOW, NOTHING EXCITING HAS HAPPENED IN A REALLY LONG TIME!"

Holy home runs, that guy needed a chill pill. He really went crazy when it came time to announce the winner of a contest that the Balmer Oreos were running. People bought raffle tickets, and the winner would receive a complete set of Major League Baseball pennants—those little flag things kids like to hang up in their rooms. A nice prize, but jeez, it's not the million-dollar sweepstakes that Mr. Spaulding acted like it was.

When they announced the winner, he just went nuts. But then, he was always going nuts. They called the winning numbers, and I was happy to see The Giant get up to claim his prize on the field during the seventh-inning stretch.

"I do not believe it! THE GIANT WINS THE PENNANTS! THE GIANT WINS THE PENNANTS! THE GIANT WINS THE PENNANTS!" Mr. Spaulding stood up and screamed at the top of his lungs.

I thought he was overly dramatic. That was, until The Giant got up to accept his prize. Where he got a microphone stand in the middle of the field, I'll never know.

"Wow," The Giant said into the microphone, his words echoing all over the park. "Who wouldn't consider this a huge honor? To be awarded these beautiful pennants? To have spent these last few seconds winning this award? Today...I consider myself...the luckiest man...on the face of the earth..."

I rolled my eyes. Jeez, it's not an Academy Award!

The rest of the seventh inning was uneventful. The only exciting thing that happened in the eighth inning was more fan interference from that stupid Jeffy Myers kid. This time, he reached over from the stands and snatched Christy's glove. I had to call time so I could go over and get it back from him.

"Dude, what gives already?" I asked Jeffy.

Jeffy held his nose. "Your team stinks. You're gonna loooose! You're gonna loooose!" he taunted.

"Possibly," I said, with unusual calm. I didn't even pop my gum. I don't know, I guess I just felt sorry for the kid for being banned from baseball. "Can I have the glove back, please?"

Jeffy stared at me for a moment, then sighed and gave it back.

"Thanks," I told him. I walked away shaking my head.

The ninth inning got a little more interesting. The umpire made a bad call against the Balmer Oreos. He called Freddie Murray out at first, but he really was safe. The Oreos manager, Pearl Weaver, came running out of the dugout to argue. She was a short, kinda heavy lady with graying hair. She pitched quite a fit, kicking the dirt and turning her hat around backward so she could get right in the umpire's face. Must be nice. It's not illegal to get mad in Balmer, so she could fight all she wanted. I had to admit she did look a little silly getting all worked up over a bad call. I supposed I'd looked just as crazy when I would lose my temper. The umpire finally tossed Pearl out of the game, which was kind of entertaining.

Joanna got walked in the ninth inning, which was cool. Except for the fact that she actually slid to base. On a walk. I know it's hard for her to ever be slow, but she had to quit sliding on walks. I mean, nobody can get you out when the pitcher walks you. You look nuts if you slide as if people are trying to get the ball to base to get you out! That, and I had to remind Christy to stop crashing unnecessarily into the wall whenever she caught the ball. She looked nuts, too.

Thanks to a home run by Tyler Corncobb, we won the game!

"GOODBYYYYYYYEEEEEE, Mr. Spaulding!" shouted one of the kids.

"Why do people always shout that to me?" asked Mr. Spaulding, shaking his big, round, baseball-shaped head as he walked away after the game.

I couldn't wait to get into the clubhouse to congratulate my guys for their big win. I was so proud of Ty I could burst! If her father had actually showed up for once, maybe he'd be proud, too. I gathered up the equipment as fast as I could so I could celebrate the win with my team. Maybe I'd take them out for ice cream. They definitely deserved it.

The moment I entered the clubhouse, I knew something was terribly, terribly wrong. The kids were all sitting on the benches. Quietly. They all looked up at me somberly. Something had definitely happened to suck the wind right out of their sails.

"Hey, now. What's the matter, guys? You won. You did a great job. You should be really proud of yourselves!" I told them.

"Is it true, Coach? It's not really true, is it?" Catfish asked.

"Is what true?" I asked. I had a horrible, sinking feeling I knew exactly what he was asking about.

"Are you really just coaching us just to keep out of jail?" Ty asked.

Oh, no....

Poor Ty. I had finally gotten her to trust me, and even to

smile and be happy once in a while. And now this. She just looked up at me, more sad than angry. Like she should have known better than to trust me.

"Well...sort of...I mean..." I had no idea what to say. My team, my kids, they all looked up at me, waiting for an explanation that I could not possibly provide. It was true. I was only coaching them because I'd felt I had no choice. I would never have agreed to coach them otherwise. At least, that was how it started. "Where did you hear that?"

"One of the kids on the Oreos," replied Carl quietly. He looked very disappointed.

"Okay, guys," I said, wearily sitting down on the bench so I could face them. "Yes, it is true. I got in trouble for getting angry one too many times. Mr. Steinbrenner really wanted me to coach because he doesn't like Mr. Hearsay." *Who does?* I felt like saying. "And he wanted to have the best chance to beat the Crankees. He always wanted me to coach the team and, well, to be honest, I really didn't want to."

The looks on my kids' faces were heartbreaking, but I wasn't finished.

"It is true I only started coaching you guys to avoid going to jail, but now I promise you I really do want to be your coach." Ty stared at her lap. She wouldn't even look up at me. "I've been having such a good time coaching you guys. You're doing so great and I'm really, really proud of you. I hope you know that." I was looking right at Ty, but she still wouldn't face me. "I guess I should have told you the truth about why I was coaching for Joyville, but I didn't want you guys to think that was the only reason I was here. I mean, that's the way it started, but I guess..."

My eyes filled up with tears. I couldn't bear their disappointed looks. Clueless looked up at me with his cute little brown eyes and freckled face. George sighed. Christy bit her lip.

"I shoulda known," Catfish said bitterly. "Ya know, I used to think it was so amazing that you were our coach. You were a legend, man. Everybody knows the great Konnie Mack was the best there ever was in Joyville. Everybody knows the stories about how great you were at baseball, and then you had to give it up when Mr. Hearsay took away the team. And it was such a big deal when you came back to baseball." He just shook his head at me. "And now we find out you didn't come back because you wanted to. You came back because you're a criminal."

I wanted to ask how the other kid on the Oreos found out about me if for no other reason than to change the subject, but I didn't. I really didn't know what to say. I looked around at my kids. Wow. Even Joanna was holding still. She was just sitting there, holding her cap in her hands. Yoyo whispered something. He looked pretty mad, so I figured I was better off that I couldn't hear what he said.

"Come on, guys," Carl said, standing up with the laundry bag. "Gimme your uniforms. I'll get 'em cleaned and ready for the next game." He didn't even look at me.

"Carl, don't worry about that. I can wash the uniforms." I told him.

"No!" Carl said sharply. "I said I'd do it."

"Yeah, I think you've done enough already," Catfish said. "Don't worry. We only have a few more games and then you'll be rid of us forever. "

They all just sat there in silence for a moment. Ty suddenly stood up. She grabbed her gym bag and stormed out of the clubhouse.

I wondered if any of them would ever forgive me.

11

I got to the field early as usual. This time, I was actually hoping some of the kids would show up early. I figured maybe if I had a chance to talk to them one at a time, maybe I could make them understand how much I really did want to be their coach and it wasn't just so I could stay out of jail.

However, instead of the kids interrupting my moment of peace and quiet on the field, the last person on the face of the planet—or any other planet for that matter ——that I wanted to see showed up. I groaned aloud as I saw Bobby Hearsay approaching. What was he doing here? We weren't even playing the Crankees! We were playing the Detail Tiggers from Detail County.

"What do you want?" I asked him irritably as he walked up to me, dressed in one of his really expensive, really ugly suits.

"Now, now. Don't lose your temper," he taunted.

"Oh, shut up," I said, and was quite satisfied with the look of shock on his face. "Dude, there's nobody here, okay?

There's nobody here to tell on me if I get mad, and you can't prove I did without somebody seeing it."

Hmmmm, I thought. Now wasn't this interesting. I really could say whatever I wanted to him and he would have no proof and no way to get me in trouble. Bobby frowned. He knew I was right. Heck, I could punch him in the gut and not get busted!

Tempting...but no way would I do it. Sure, I lost my temper sometimes, but I'm not the type to go punching people out no matter how much they might happen to deserve it.

"Tsk, tsk, tsk. Just like you, Konnie. Always angry. I feel bad for your team. You're not good for them at all." He shook his head, pretending to look sad. "You set such a bad example for them."

"Oh, and you set a good example, I suppose? By cheating? What did you do, pay the umpires to blow calls against my team?" I asked him.

He pretended to look shocked. "Why, Miss MacDonald, I can't believe you would say such a thing! Well, actually, I can't believe you were smart enough to figure it out on your own."

My chest tightened. My fists curled. *Pop*! I popped my gum, took a deep breath, tried to count to ten. I used all the tricks I could think of to calm myself down. My parents taught me not to hate anybody, so let's just say I disliked Bobby Hearsay more than I'd ever disliked anybody else in the whole wide world.

"I don't even know why you bother trying to beat my team anyway. You've got one more game against us this season, and if I were you, I wouldn't bother to show up. What's the point? Your team stinks."

"They do not!" I shouted. I quickly looked around.

Thankfully, there was still nobody around because that outburst alone was enough to get me taken away in handcuffs.

"Please. They're awful!"

"No, they're not. They've won some games," I said, thinking of how hard my team tried and how well they'd been doing lately.

"Ha!" Bobby said. He laughed and shook his head. "Against who. Stan Musical's team? What a joke!"

Well, he had me there. Sure, we had beaten the Blu Rays, but that hardly counted. A pack of stray dogs could beat that team. And I bet the dogs would run the bases in the right order, too.

"We also beat the Balmer Oreos," I informed him.

A flicker of surprise flashed across Bobby's face. It was quick, but I was able to catch it before it turned back into a scowl. "Yeah. Big deal. So did we."

"Yeah, but we didn't have to pay anybody to get our win."

Zing!

Ooooh, that one got him good. Heehee. It was really fun watching his nostrils flare.

"Stan's a total wuss..." I said.

"Agreed!" Bobby said, and was probably just as amazed as me that we agreed on anything.

"But why hasn't Pearl ever ratted you out for cheating?" I asked.

He snorted. "Oh, she's such a hothead. She tried telling on me once, but she's always yellin' and kickin' dirt at the umpires, so nobody believed her. The Judge Mann just sent her on her merry way."

"That must have ticked her off," I thought, picturing how mad Pearl must have been. So unfair that she was allowed to get mad, even at The Judge Mann, because the rules were different in Balmer. The Judge Mann was the judge for all the towns around here, but even he couldn't bust Pearl for throwing an angry tantrum in Balmer.

"Speaking of being ticked off..." Bobby said, grinning at me. "I bet your kids weren't too happy when they found out the real reason you're their coach."

"How did you know that my kids found out about..." I began, and then felt stupid for not having figured it out sooner. It was Bobby's fault my kids knew about my criminal past. Sure, it had been one of the Balmer Oreos who had told them, but I was sure now that Bobby had told his team and they had blabbed to the other players. It was just a matter of time until somebody told the Joyville team.

"Those poor little dears," Bobby said, shaking his head and acting like he really cared about my team. "They must have been so disappointed when they found out you never wanted to be their coach. But, I'm sure they were super honored that you chose them over jail, eh?" Bobby said, nudging me with his elbow.

"Oh, I'm sure they were," I said. Then I nudged him back so hard he almost fell into the dirt. Darn. If only I'd nudged him just an eensy bit harder...

"Really doesn't matter who their coach is, now, does it? I mean, seriously, Konnie, I know you're good. I remember watching you in the glory days of Joyville. You know, before I came in and bought the team and took them to Cranksville?"

I gritted my teeth. "Yes. Yes, I remember..." Of course I did. It was one of the worst days of my life. I'll never forget waking up that day and hearing all over the news that Bobby Hearsay had stolen baseball from Joyville like the Grinch had stolen Christmas. "I remember you were a heck of a ballplayer," he said.

"The best. I was the best baseball player Joyville had ever seen," I informed him flatly.

"Yes, well. Be that as it may...there's only so much you can do with a bunch of losers like your team. I mean, man. They are awful!"

My temper flared dangerously. Anger boiled up in the pit of my stomach. I wanted to shove Bobby into the dirt and then kick him while he was down. Then I'd watch him cry over the damage I'd done to his horrible suit.

"They're not awful." I said, my voice cracking as I tried not to cry. "They *were* awful and that's only because they didn't know anything about baseball, which was all your fault." I said, pointing my finger at his chest. "They'd never even seen a baseball game, so of course they didn't know how to play. So I taught them how to play. I *taught* them. And not just because of the jail thing. I taught them because I want them to love the game as much as I do." My eyes brimmed over with tears. Oh, how I really, really hated crying in front of him.

"Aww, that's cute. You've become attached to those little losers! Such a shame," Bobby said. He looked at me and laughed. "A *crying* shame, apparently. Just when those dumb kids were starting to like you, they had to find out the truth. Now they think you don't care about them. Especially that little brat, Ty. Now she knows you don't care at all about her. Just like her own father."

BAM!

Holy home runs, I punched Bobby Hearsay in the face.

He landed in the dirt, ruining his fancy-schmancy suit.

Wow. Seeing him lying there in the dirt where a dirty dog like him belonged was even better than I had imagined, and I had been imagining it *a lot*. I barely had time to enjoy it when I heard a gasp come from nearby.

Ty just stood there, mouth open and staring at us. Bobby on the ground and me with my punching fist still in the air. Ty locked eyes with me before running off into the clubhouse.

Well. So much for no witnesses. But she wouldn't tell on me.

Would she?

12

As I sat in the middle of the courtroom, I still could not believe Ty had told on me. I knew she was mad. Of course she was. I understood that, and she had every right to be angry, but I still couldn't believe she would actually go tell The Judge Mann I had gotten into a fight. Seriously, who hadn't wanted to punch Bobby Hearsay in the face?

I was hardly even listening to the Judge. What was the point? I knew exactly what the sentence would be because he had said so during my last trial. If I got mad again, it was five years in the Joyville jail.

Wow. Five years.

Ty must have known what my punishment would be. I'm sure Bobby told those awful Crankees the whole story. No matter how mad she was, how could Ty tell on me knowing it meant I'd have to spend five years in jail?

"You're here because you violated the agreement we had last time," The Judge Mann began gleefully. "And you know what that means!" He winked at me. Wow. I had forgotten how much he hated me. This must be the happiest day of his life. Finally getting the chance to throw me in jail.

I was kinda surprised I wasn't more upset. I didn't have much family in Joyville. Just my mom. And I didn't really have any friends, especially now, since my whole team hated me. There was one thing I did have going for me in jail. Something that had been out of my life for far, far too long.

"They got a baseball team in jail now, right, Judge?" I asked, popping my gum at him for good measure. His annoying smile disappeared. They couldn't keep us in the jail cell all day. They had to let us out for exercise, and I knew for a fact that the inmates had formed a team. I might have to go to jail, but I could still play baseball. That was all that really mattered to me. Now that I'd gotten back into baseball, I wasn't ever going to let go of it again.

"Yes," The Judge Mann admitted grouchily. "Yes, they do..."

I smiled. The idea that I'd get to do what I loved most while being in jail made him really mad.

Good.

"Anyway," the judge said, clearing his throat. He raised his gavel to make my jail sentence final, but he didn't seem quite as gleeful as he had a moment ago. I had taken all the fun out of his finally being able to lock me up. Ha! Good.

"Wait, wait!" shouted Gabe, bursting into the courtroom just like he had the first time. I wondered why he didn't just show up on time when my trial started. I guess he wanted to make a dramatic entrance. "Please don't send Konnie to jail!"

"Hah!" The Judge Mann snorted. No way was he going to let Gabe Steinbrenner cheat him out of another chance to send me to jail. I knew exactly why Gabe showed up here today trying to rescue me. He still hadn't given up hope that I would be able to get the Joyville Sweat Sox to beat the Cranksville Crankees. Forget it, dude. There was no way. Even if I wasn't in jail, Bobby would just cheat and lie and win anyway. It was totally pointless.

"Please. You've got to let her out. Just for one game. I swear! Just for one game. Let Konnie lead her team against the Crankees and then you can throw her right back in jail," Mr. Steinbrenner said.

"Hey!" I said. "Why should I help you if you're just gonna throw me back in the clink?" Sheesh. He wasn't even trying to save me from my punishment.

"Please, Judge!" Gabe pleaded. It was kinda pathetic. Still, part of me couldn't blame him. I understood exactly how it felt to want to beat Bobby Hearsay. That was kinda why I punched his lights out.

"Tell you what..." The Judge Mann said, leaning over the bench to look down his glasses at Gabe. "I'll strike you a deal, see? I'll let Konnie off the hook—completely—as in NO prison sentence at all, and she goes free..."

"What?" I asked, astonished. I couldn't believe what I was hearing!

"If she plays that game against the Cranksville Crankees...and wins."

I rolled my eyes. Darn. I'd gotten my hopes up that I just might be off the hook. There was no way—absolutely none—that we could possibly win against Bobby's team. The sad part was, if they actually played fairly, we might have had a shot.

My team was just as good, if not better, than those awful Crankees. It would have been a pretty good match, putting those teams together to see who came out on top. But Bobby

Hearsay would just cheat all the way. Accuse my team of being too old, like Carl, or too blond or too fat or whatever crime he accused them of. Not to mention the fact that he paid off the umpires to make bad calls against us. It was impossible to win, but if Gabe really wanted me to try, then I would. Whatever. It would at least give me one last time to see my team, even if none of them were speaking to me.

"What the heck. Why not? One more game on the outside before joining the Joyville Prison team."

"Great!" Mr. Steinbrenner said, practically jumping up and down with excitement.

The Judge Mann wasn't about to let me go quite that easily. Peering over his glasses at me, he added "However! If she gets mad at the game, she will spend *ten* years in prison..."

I sucked in a breath and let it out. Wow. Ten years was a really, really long time. I knew I had to keep cool at that game, no matter what.

"Fine. Cool. Whatever," I said.

"I'm not finished!" The Judge Mann roared. This time, his voice actually scared me. He wasn't kidding around. He was seriously angry. I thought this might be a bad time to point out he was breaking the law, so I kept my big mouth shut. "If Konnie's team wins the game, she gets off scot-free," he said, sounding as if those words were a bitter poison sliding down his throat. "But if she loses..." he said, peering down his nose and looking directly at me, "then Konnie MacDonald will be banned from playing baseball. Forever."

I gasped. I was about to scream out, to shout that I'd rather go to jail for the rest of my life than be banned from baseball. That, for me, a lifetime ban from the game I loved was far worse than a life sentence.

"Deal!" said Mr. Steinbrenner before I even had a chance to speak.

Bang! went The Judge Mann's gavel, making my punishment official.

13

I got to L.O.S.E.R. field super-early this time. I just had to make sure I had at least a few moments to myself.

Because I knew this was gonna be my last time on a baseball field. I knew I would cry, so I wanted to get it all out of my system before the kids or Bobby Hearsay showed up.

My kids.

It was gonna be hard to get through this game with them hating me so much. I knew we wouldn't win, but what if they refused to even try? They didn't know what would happen to me if we lost, and there was no way I was going to tell them. I couldn't bear the thought of them blaming themselves for my fate if we lost. Let them just think this was an ordinary baseball game.

I still loved my kids and I tried really, really hard not to be mad at Ty. How could she have done this to me? I couldn't help but wonder how she would feel if she knew I'd only punched Bobby Hearsay for saying bad stuff about her.

No.

There was no reason for her to know about that. Ty was

just a kid. She wasn't a bad kid. She was just disappointed in me. I had disappointed her just like her father always did.

I wondered what my father would say about my being banned from baseball for life. I tried not to think about it.

Catfish was the first one to show up. It still made me smile to see him wearing that pink jersey. I felt the tears coming again as I thought about how much I would miss these guys. I wiped my eyes quickly as I watched him walk over to me.

"Hi, Coach," Catfish said shyly. He didn't seem mad at me anymore. "Glad you got busted out of jail."

I nodded. "Yeah. Me too."

"We were really worried about you. We were afraid you were gonna get locked up for a long time. That was a close one!"

Yep. He definitely had no idea what was riding on this game. He thought they'd just let me go. Not even close. If I lost this game, I was banned from baseball forever. Plus, if I got mad again, I'd go to jail for ten whole years.

"Of all people to rat you out," Catfish said with a look of disgust.

"I know. I still can't believe Ty would do that."

Catfish's eyes grew wide. "Ty? Is that who you think sold you out?"

"Yeah. She was the only one around when I punched Bobby."

"Oh man, Ty would never do that. Never! Not to anybody and especially not to you. You're like her hero."

"I am?" I asked, astonished. I felt good and terrible at the same time. Good that I was her hero and terrible that I had let her down so badly.

"Does the name Casey Thayer mean anything to you?" Catfish asked.

Casey Thayer, Casey Thayer. Yes, the name sounded familiar but I couldn't quite place it. I knew that name from somewhere.

"He's the one who ratted you out."

"That jerk! Um, who is he?"

"He's Bobby Hearsay's cousin, that's who. You know him as the guy who cuts the grass," Catfish said.

The Giant....

"No way!" I shouted.

"Yes, way! He was spying on us all that time. Whenever he was here, he was watching us and reporting back to Mr. Hearsay like a little snitch."

"Wow. Unbelievable."

"I know," Catfish said, shaking his head. "And Casey wasn't even here when you punched Mr. Hearsay. He was over cleaning up the Oreos' field! He just said he was there 'cause Mr. Hearsay told him to lie and say he saw it. I heard them talking about it when they didn't know I was listening." He shook his head, and then looked up me. "Coach?"

"Yeah?"

"I sure wish I'd been there to see you hit that guy."

I burst out laughing.

"The guys have really missed you."

"Really?"

"Really," he said with a grin.

I waited until all kids had assembled in the clubhouse, then I went inside. They all stood up and started clapping for me. Oh, no. Here came the tears again.

"Oh, don't cry!" Brooke said, jumping up. She grabbed a tissue and started dabbing at my eyes. "You'll smear your makeup!"

"Relax, Coach," Carl said, finally smiling again. "Here,

have a cookie." He opened up the tin of cookies he had brought for us.

"Thanks, Carl. Delicious, as always," I said, after taking a bite and brushing the crumbs off my rainbow jersey.

"Here, have a sip of this," Joanna offered helpfully. She handed me her squeeze bottle of water.

One sip and I realized too late that it was not water that Joanna had kept in her bottle. The liquid was lukewarm and very bitter. It took all my effort not to spit the contents across the room. I managed to swallow it before croaking, "What is this?"

Joanna smiled and cheerfully replied "Fielder's Choice coffee."

Coffee. So that was what she was always drinking. Holy home runs, no wonder she was forever acting like a puppy with springs in its butt. Who could sit still after downing that much caffeine? I'd turn cartwheels all day too if I drank this stuff all day long.

Yoyo got up from the bench and put his arm around me. He whispered something that sounded like, "It's okay, Coach."

"What did you say?" I asked him.

From across the room, Catfish stood up. "He said we're not mad, Coach. We understand. The laws in Joyville are dumb. It should be okay to get mad. Everybody gets mad sometimes. We're still glad that you're our coach and we think you are totally the best."

"You sure he said all that?" I asked, raising an eyebrow. Yoyo shrugged, and then nodded as if to say even if he didn't say all that stuff, he still agreed with it.

I looked out at all my kids smiling up at me. A huge feeling of relief washed over me. They had found out the truth, and they weren't mad anymore.

"Listen, guys," I said in a serious voice. They all hushed up to hear what I had to say. I had to figure out a way to let them know the importance of winning this game without them finding out what was truly riding on it. "I can't tell you how important it is that we win this game."

"Are you serious?" Catfish asked. "I mean, you know that's impossible, right? With Mr. Hearsay—"

"I know, I know," I said, sighing, wearily rubbing my temples. "But we have to try because..."

I looked at Clueless, smiling up at me with his adorable face. I saw Christy grinning, braids swinging. I saw Joanna hopping from foot to foot, tossing the baseball back and forth in her hands, excited to play. Yoyo smiled and whispered something. I had no idea what it was, but I was sure it was something nice because he was a sweet kid. Ty looked at me, too. I couldn't tell if she was still mad at me or not, but she did seem to be listening.

"Yeah, Coach? Because..." Catfish asked.

"Because *nothing,*" I said defiantly. Right then and there I made a decision. Maybe there was no way we could possibly win, but we sure as heck could have fun. And that was what I wanted for these kids. They'd worked so hard all season. Whether they won or lost, they always had a great attitude and tremendous team spirit. They wore those ridiculous uniforms with pride, no matter how many other kids called them Power Rangers or Care Bears or whatever. "We're gonna go out there and have the most fun any team ever had playing baseball!"

The kids whooped and yelled. They jumped off the benches, fired up. They were excited to play. They always were.

I shook my head and said softly, "All this time, I've been telling you to respect the game...and you do respect the game. You have from the very beginning. Because loving the game *is* respecting the game..."

Clueless grinned at me and nodded, holding two thumbs up. This time, I simply couldn't resist it...I pinched his cheeks.

"You are so cute!" I told him. He just laughed good-naturedly.

"Okay," I said. "New rule."

I grabbed a red dry-erase marker and put a giant X through all the rules that I had told them to follow since the first day. I wrote just one rule for them to follow.

Love the game.

"Yes, Coach," Catfish said, and the other kids nodded happily.

"I know what we need for this last game," I said, trying not to let my voice crack when I said the word *last*. The kids thought it was just the last game of the season. They had no idea it would be my last game ever. I reached into my locker and pulled out a very special wooden baseball. Wonderball.

When I saw George's face light up, I knew this would all be worthwhile. One last, amazing game before I was forced to hang up my cleats for good.

"Wow...really? We can use Wonderball?" George asked me hopefully.

"You bet we can!" I told him. I pinched his chubby cheeks, too.

"Something else we need...Carl!"

"Yeah, Coach?" Carl asked.

"Go get Teddy Williams. We'll need him for good luck."

"Wow! Cool! Okay!" Carl said and rushed to get his teddy bear.

"I don't want Teddy Williams to be lonely, so let's bring a friend, too," I said. I pulled out my stuffed elephant from my locker. “I want everybody to meet Philly the Elephant. He was a gift from my dad.”

“That’s nice,” Ty said softly. She smiled at me. In that moment, I knew she had forgiven me. What a great kid.

“Ty,” I said to her.

“Yeah, Coach?”

“Don’t wait for your dad to show up today, okay? He’s not coming.”

Ty looked stunned by my blunt words. I might as well have slapped her in the face. I walked over to her, sat down, and slung my arm around her. “I’m not trying to be mean. It’s just that I can’t bear to see that look of disappointment on your face anymore. I know you want your dad to be proud of you. But please, please know I could not be more proud of you if you were my own daughter. And to tell you the truth, I wish you were.”

Tears filled Ty’s eyes. She wrapped her arms around me and said, “Thank you, Konnie.”

“Hey. We’re all proud of her, aren’t we, guys?” Catfish said loudly.

Shouts of agreement came from all the kids. One kid shouted louder than anybody else.

“WE ARE SUPER-DUPER-DUPER PROUD OF YOU, TY!”

We all looked up in astonishment.

It was Yoyo.

“Hey, I only speak up when I got something important to say,” Yoyo said softly, but not quite a whisper. Ty rewarded him with a big bear hug.

“So, are we ready to take on the Crankees?”

“YEAH!!”

“I want you all to have fun out there!” I shouted at the top of my lungs. “Joanna, slide on walks if you want to!

Christy, crash into the wall in the outfield if you want to!" Then I pointed at her. "Just don't get hurt... Clueless or Shoeless Joe, you don't have to wear shoes if you don't want to!"

"Thanks! But I wanna wear shoes. Because I believe in the sole. The sole, the shoe, the cleat. I believe in the Wonderball, Teddy Williams, Philly the Elephant, and I believe there should be a law against jerks like Mr. Hearsay!" Clueless informed me.

"Agreed! Are we ready? Hands in Joyville. On three. One-two-three- GO SWEAT SOX!"

We walked out on the field together. I stopped suddenly.

"You okay, Coach?" Ty asked, looking concerned.

"Yeah. I just thought of something. Something else to make this game complete."

The kids watched as I strode over to center field. I walked all the way over to where the fans were waiting for the game to start. Jeffy Myers started taunting me the minute I got near him.

"You're gonna loooose, you're gonna—"

I covered his mouth with my hand. "I want you to come play with us."

Jeffy's eyes got huge. "You mean it?"

I nodded. "It's not right that anybody should ever be banned from playing the great game of baseball. Come with me."

Jeffy grabbed his glove—and he had quite a pile to choose from since he'd been stealing them from outfielders all these years—and hopped over the fence to join our team.

When we joined the rest of the Joyville lineup for the national anthem, Catfish smiled at me. He nodded, apparently approving of my decision to let Jeffy join our team.

After all, the only rule was to love the game. And I knew Jeffy did.

I was bursting with pride as I watched my kids stand with their colorful caps over their hearts during the national anthem.

The game began with a bang. Catfish struck out the first three batters. Then we were up to bat. Once again, first-pitch swinging, Brooke hit it out of the park. With one pitch, Joyville was up 1-0. My heart soared. Was there hope after all? Was it possible to beat the Crankees and save my life in baseball?

When George got up to bat, Bobby Hearsay came running over before the pitcher could even start his windup. What now?

"Violation! Rule violation!" Bobby shouted. How could George have violated a rule? He was just standing there. "He's got too much pine tar on his bat. You're not allowed to have that much pine tar on the bat!"

The umpire came running up to inspect the bat.

"It's not pine tar," George said. He ran his finger down the bat, and then licked his finger. "It's chocolate!"

The umpire shook his head, and then winked at Bobby. "I'm sorry. No chocolate allowed on the bats. You're outta the game!"

"No, that's not fair!" I said.

"Are you getting mad, Miss MacDonald?" Bobby asked, grinning at me.

I swallowed and looked at George. He looked terribly disappointed that he would have to leave the game, but he put a supportive hand on my back. He knew I couldn't get angry without getting in trouble. He knew there was nothing I could do.

"It's okay, Coach," he said. He wearily went back to sit on

the Johnny Bench. Good thing I had Jeffy, or we might have had to forfeit if we lost any more players.

Bobby continued to cheat throughout the game, but I really had to give my kids credit. They never let it get them down. At one point, Joanna had a hit and dashed to base. The Crankees first baseman bobbled the ball, but of course the umpire called Joanna out.

Catfish shouted, "You dropped the ball twice and it took you twenty minutes to pick it up. The runner could be halfway to Mexico by now. No, she's not out!" The umpire just made the out sign again. Catfish laughed and waved him off. All the players could see what a joke the game was and how obvious it was that Bobby was cheating, but nobody bothered to stand up to him.

Things were fine, more or less, until the eighth inning or so. Suddenly, the whole mood of the game seemed to change. I couldn't understand it. At first, the kids just laughed off the Crankees' awful, cheating ways. They just accepted there was nothing anybody could do so they might as well just have fun.

Then, all of a sudden, the kids weren't laughing anymore. Catfish looked deadly serious as he prepared to pitch. He and Yoyo had several secret meetings on the mound to discuss strategy. Ty kept shooting me worried looks from her place at first base. Joanna was quieter than I'd ever seen her. Instead of bouncing around like a nut, she was stone still as she prepared to field the ball if it came her way. Even little Clueless looked serious instead of smiling. It suddenly hit me.

They knew.

One of those Crankees had told them about my sentence. They knew I would be banned from playing baseball for the rest of my life if we lost this game, so they were giving it everything they had to try to win for me.

My whole body flooded with emotions. My heart ached when I thought about having to leave baseball behind forever, but I was so filled with warmth and peace at the thought that these kids cared for me as much I as did for them. I felt a lump in my throat when I realized my dad would be so proud of them. Of me. These kids were so amazing. They knew it was almost certainly impossible to win this game but they were trying the best they could anyway, and it was all to help me. I wanted to rush onto the field and hug each and every one of them. I knew there would be time for that after the game. Before...before I had to leave the field for the last time. I would hug them and hold onto them until The Judge Mann forced me to let go.

I watched as Catfish wound up to pitch. His form was amazing. I couldn't believe how far he had come since he was that wild boy who couldn't even hit the dugout wall. He struck out Arod Rodriguez on three pitches. Thank goodness the kid actually swung through them all. Otherwise the umpire would have called every pitch a ball even if it sailed right through the strike zone. The people in the stands could see him swinging, so even the lying umpires couldn't say he didn't strike out. Bobby and the umpires were careful enough not to make their cheating obvious enough that the spectators could tell what they were up to. Only the players and their managers knew for sure.

It came down to the bottom of the ninth. We were losing 2-1. It was so close that I could hardly bear it, but I felt worse for my kids. They were playing their hearts out. They would never forgive themselves if they lost this game, which wasn't fair because it wasn't their fault! How could they possibly beat Bobby Hearsay? How could anybody?

I glanced out into the stands and saw my mom, chewing on her nails, fretting. She knew how critical this game was for me. I thought of Ty, and realized how lucky I was to have had two parents who loved and supported me. I knew my dad was watching over me now.

Jeffy managed to get on base. I was so excited for him! He ran to first base and jumped up and down. There was sheer joy on his face. He wasn't a bad kid. He just harassed everybody and told them they stunk because he felt so bad about being banned from baseball. I think that's true of a lot of mean people. They're not always mean. Sometimes they're just sad.

Believe me. I know.

We had Jeffy on base. We had two outs. Ty stepped up to the plate. Oh, if she could just get on base, we could stay alive. We actually had a shot at winning!

I held my breath.

Strike one.

Strike two...

Oh, no...

On the third pitch, she connected with the ball. She connected *good.* The crowd jumped to their feet. I heard Mr. Spaulding screaming, but then he was always screaming. The ball was going, going, going...

GONE.

Two-run home run.

We'd won the game.

Ty yelled and waved her hands as she ran the bases. After she and Jeffy had both crossed the plate, the Joyville Sweat Sox all collapsed in a heap. We were hugging and crying and yelling. It was wonderful.

But it didn't last.

The next thing I knew, I saw Bobby and the umpire charging toward me.

I saw Bobby's awful smile, and I knew it was all over.

"It was foul," Bobby said. "It doesn't count."

"You...you can't be serious! Everyone in the park saw—"

Bobby just shook his head. The umpire made the "to the right" motion, meaning the ball was foul. The crowd groaned and sat back down to resume the game. I knew then it was completely hopeless. No matter what happened, Bobby was going to win. In the background, I faintly heard Mr. Steinbrenner's voice. He was firing Wee Willy again, somehow blaming this loss on him.

And then it happened.

I got angry.

I got angrier than I'd ever been in my entire life. I'd had enough of Bobby Hearsay and his awful, lying ways. I'd had enough of his evil smile and the way he treated my precious kids. Let him do what he wanted to me, but no way was I about to let him get away with hurting Ty like that. She was my game-winning hero. I wasn't letting him take that away without a fight.

That's right. *A fight.*

"NO WAY, BOBBY! NO WAY ARE YOU GETTING AWAY WITH THIS!" I screamed at him in front of everybody. I didn't care who saw me get mad. I was way past caring about anything but my kids anymore. I was panting, practically breathless, as blood surged through my body. Remembering Pearl Weaver, I turned my cap around so I could scream right in his face. I punctuated my words with sharp finger jabs in his chest.

"YOU'RE...NOT...GETTING...AWAY...WITH... THIS!

Bobby looked stunned at first, but then he smiled his

little snobby bank-manager smile. He was thrilled that he had gotten me mad.

"That was a home run and you know it! Everybody saw Tyler Corncobb hit that ball all the way outta the park!"

"No way," Bobby said calmly, casually straightening out his suit from where I'd rumpled it with my finger jabbing. "It was too high."

"Too high? What does that even mean, too high? It was a GAME WINNING, TWO-RUN HOME-RUN YOU STUPID JERK!"

I kicked dirt at him. I picked up home plate and threw it for good measure. When I turned around, a horrible sight reached my eyes.

The Judge Mann was charging toward me with handcuffs.

"Oh no, please," I whimpered. "Not in front of my kids." For the rest of their lives they would have nightmares of seeing me carted away in handcuffs, and they would probably blame themselves. Oh, I should have known The Judge Mann was gonna come to this game. He wouldn't want to miss watching me lose.

The Judge Mann charged toward me.

Then he charged *past* me.

And slapped the handcuffs on Bobby Hearsay.

The crowd gasped. Nobody gasped louder than me.

"I told the truth about him." I turned around to see Stan Musical standing behind me. "I'm really sorry I didn't do it sooner. It wasn't right, what he was doing to the game, to the kids. So I told The Judge Mann."

"Don't you know who I am!" sputtered Bobby Hearsay, shocked at the turn of events.

"Yep. You're a liar and a cheat," said The Judge Mann, "and I'm afraid that's against the law. Even when you live in

Cranksville." He turned to me. "I know we've had our differences over the years, Miss Konnie Mack, but you've done good with those kids. The way you were always yelling and cheering them on no matter what. I saw a lot of your father in you today."

I didn't know what to say. That was the nicest thing that anybody could possibly say to me. I tried to choke back my tears. "Then...then...I can still play baseball?"

The Judge Mann nodded. "I wouldn't dream of taking a great player like you out of the game. And maybe, just maybe...I need to reconsider this No Anger Law. I mean, everybody gets mad once in a while, right?"

"Y-yes. Yes, sir. That's true!"

The Judge Mann shot a disgusted look at Bobby. "After the way he treated your kids today, what kind of coach would you be if you didn't get mad? You were right to do what you did, Konnie."

"Thank you. Thank you, sir!"

The Judge Mann actually smiled at me. I think it made him happy that I finally showed him some respect and called him "sir". I also think seeing Bobby's antics on the field today reminded him that maybe I wasn't a criminal just because I got mad sometimes. Other people were a lot worse by comparison.

The Judge Mann cleared his throat. "So, in my official capacity as judge, I judge that was a two-run homer. Joyville wins!"

The crowd went wild. My kids all came running up to me, tackling me to the ground. From underneath the pile of kids practically smothering me, I could hear my mom cheering for me in the stands.

"Okay, okay, don't kill me!" They finally let me up, and I gave each and every one of them a hug. I held onto them like I'd never let go. Thanks to The Judge Mann, now I wouldn't have to.

"Now, go get changed so we can go out for ice cream!"

"Great! I want coffee-flavored!" shouted Joanna.

I quietly followed the kids to the clubhouse. I wanted to watch them open their lockers. There was a surprise in there for them, but it was no red tag this time.

I watched happily as each kid opened their locker and found their own, personal baseball card. I'd gotten great pictures of them throughout the season. Catfish, grinning like a goof in his pink jersey. Ty, looking serious as she worked at first base. Clueless with his sweet smile. Joanna turning a cartwheel. As each kid discovered their card, they smiled. I watched happily as they showed each other what they got.

Wow.

I couldn't wait until next year.

14

I had thought spring would never get here, but it finally came. The smell of the fresh-cut grass and the dirt of the field took my breath away, like it always did. This time, it wasn't the threat of jail that made me coach for Joyville. I knew now that not coaching, not playing baseball again would be worse than jail.

I couldn't believe how much my kids had grown since last year! I thought Carl couldn't possibly get any taller, but somehow he had. I didn't think George could possibly get any...I mean, he's still a big boy. I hadn't seen most of the kids since last summer.

Except for Ty. She and I hung out a lot together. We practiced baseball all year long. At the batting cages in the winter and on the field when it was nice. Her father still ignored her, but it seemed to bother her less than it used to. It wasn't right, but she knew she couldn't change it.

I was tired of seeing poor Wee Willy Martin get fired, so I'd offered him a position with more job security. He was my new assistant coach.

Bobby Hearsay is still in jail where he belongs. He's allowed to play baseball, but not even the prisoners will play with him. As for me, I'm ready to play some ball.

Pop!

THANK YOU!

Thank you for reading this book! I would be so grateful if you would take the time (or help your child) to leave a review of *The Joyville Sweat Sox*. Reviews are vital to any author's success.

I would love to hear from you! You can contact me at lindafausnet@gmail.com.

ACKNOWLEDGMENTS

Heartfelt thanks to all who contributed to making this book happen. Thanks to Beth Miller, Kendall Bailey, and Zann Wasiljov for their helpful and honest beta reads of the book. Thanks to my parents for their support and for taking me to baseball games as a kid. Special thanks to my sister, Zann, who shares my love of baseball. We've had many baseball-related travel adventures, and here's to many more!

Thanks to my husband, Bill, and my children, Celia and Noah, for their love and support and for tolerating my screaming at the TV when the Orioles are losing.

www.ingramcontent.com/pod-product-compliance
Lightning Source LLC
Chambersburg PA
CBHW071557040426
42452CB00008B/1199